Salomon Jadassohn, Gustav Tyson-Wolff, E.M. Barber

A Manual of Simple, Double, Triple and Quadruple

Counterpoint

Salomon Jadassohn, Gustav Tyson-Wolff, E.M. Barber

A Manual of Simple, Double, Triple and Quadruple Counterpoint

ISBN/EAN: 9783337198398

Printed in Europe, USA, Canada, Australia, Japan

Cover: Foto ©Andreas Hilbeck / pixelio.de

More available books at **www.hansebooks.com**

MANUAL

OF

SIMPLE, DOUBLE, TRIPLE AND QUADRUPLE

COUNTERPOINT

BY

S. JADASSOHN,

PROFESSOR AT THE ROYAL CONSERVATORIUM OF MUSIC, LEIPZIG.

TRANSLATED INTO ENGLISH

BY

GUSTAV (TYSON-) WOLFF,

MUS. DOC. CANTUAR.

THIRD EDITION,

REVISED BY E. M. BARBER.

LEIPZIG, BREITKOPF AND HÄRTEL

NEW-YORK, G. SCHIRMER.

ENTᴰ STA. HALL.

1897.

PREFACE.

The subsequent Manual contains instructions for the study of simple, double, triple and quadruple Counterpoint. All the rules, principles and remarks set forth in this volume, are founded on the contrapuntal works of BACH, HÄNDEL, and other classical masters, who have written in our system of the major and minor keys.

These studies in Counterpoint are intended to prepare the student for the composition of Canon and Fugue; but those also, who do not intend to become musicians by profession, will be enabled to penetrate more deeply into the works of the classical masters and to cope with the difficulties of their sublime creations. Let no one imagine, however, that the knowledge of the rules alone would suffice; these would be attained quickly and with little trouble. Only serious, conscientious study can further the pupil here, as well as in all other branches of art. Only when the student has mastered all the problems contained in this book in a thorough manner, will he be enabled to proceed to the study of Canon and Fugue.

Leipzig.

Dr. S. Jadassohn.

PREFACE TO THE SECOND EDITION.

The English translation to the second edition of my Manual of Counterpoint has been revised and corrected in accordance with my special request and under my immediate supervision by my highly gifted pupil, Mr. E. M. BARBER of London.

It clearly and conscientiously represents the German text. I give my hearty thanks to Mr. BARBER, a very excellent musician, for his intelligent assistance and I hope that this revised translation will enable the pupil to understand completely all the rules, principles and remarks contained in my work.

Leipzig, November 1891.

Dr. S. Jadassohn.

REVISER'S PREFACE TO THE SECOND EDITION.

The correction of the first edition was only undertaken at the special request of the author; as his pupil, I personally felt the necessity for a clearer and better translation; this was moreover strengthened by the opinions I heard expressed on all sides.

I have endeavoured to preserve unaltered the respected author's views as expressed in the German text; at the same time seeking to clothe them with the correct English technical terms.

In conclusion, I wish to thank Dr. JADASSOHN for his kindness and forbearance in repeatedly giving me the fullest explanations; and trust the result will prove useful alike to himself and his other pupils.

Leipzig, Nov. 1891.

E. M. Barber.

PREFACE TO THE THIRD EDITION.

The third edition of the »Manual of Counterpoint« is issued according to the second edition. The later published and separately edited »Exercises and Examples for the studies in Counterpoint« forming an essential completition to the »Manual« are mostly instructive and may be recommended to teachers and pupils.

Leipzig, June 1897.

Dr. S. Jadassohn.

CONTENTS.

PART THIRD.

PART FIRST.
Simple Counterpoint.

CHAPTER I.

Note against Note.

§ 1. The term Counterpoint implies the independent progression of one or more melodious parts or voices with one another, taking into consideration a natural and correct connection of chords.

Melody is therefore the characteristic feature of Counterpoint; each of the parts or melodies thus united, must be worked out independently; each must be a perfectly constituted part of the whole. This enables us to change at will, the relative position of the parts in double, triple and quadruple counterpoint. Thus each part in its turn may become soprano, alto, tenor, or bass.

We have already recommended to the student in the exercises in our book on Harmony, (where we dealt with the structure and connection of chords,) a greater amount of care and consideration, in the progression of parts from a melodious point of view. In the last exercises in the "Manual of Harmony" particular attention was called to the formation of bass and soprano. Referring to this, we can at once begin with the exercises in simple counterpoint. We make a distinction between *Simple Counterpoint* in Note against Note, in which only notes of equal duration are placed to a cantus firmus, — and *Florid Counterpoint*, in which two or more notes are placed in one, or several parts against the cantus firmus. In the former the progression of parts will be independent only with respect to melody; but in florid counterpoint, the progression will be independent in a rhythmical, as well as a melodic respect.

The only difference then, between the exercises in simple counterpoint, and our last studies in the "Manual of Harmony" is that the choice of the harmony employed is now free. By this means the opportunity is given of bestowing especial attention to a more melodious progression of each individual part.

We commence our exercises as before in four-parts, and place the cantus firmus in the bass, to which the student will have to find the three upper parts. He should treat these in different ways, with respect to position and choice of chords. It is intended that the student should only employ diatonic chords for the first few exercises, choosing at first as simple harmonies as possible, and only allow himself by degrees the more rarely used harmonies. After the cantus firmus has been worked out several times with diatonic harmonies, he will then be allowed to employ modulations but these however must not lead too far, nor be introduced in an unnatural, or forced manner. The treatment of the subjoined bass may serve as further explanation.

Cantus firmus.

Note. The student is recommended to work his exercises always in the four clefs. The following examples are printed on two merely to save space.

In the above example, only the six notes of the 2nd 3d 4th 5th 6th 7th bars allow a change of harmony; the chord of the first and last bar must necessarily be the triad of the tonic: the chord of the last bar but one must, as Dominant, prepare the close. Nevertheless this cantus firmus allows a great number of different ways of treatment. The first two of the above examples contain only common chords; in the third and eighth we find the chord of the Dominant Seventh; in the 4th 5th 6th 7th 14th 15th and 16th examples, diatonic chords of the seventh are used; in the 9th and 10th examples, we find the secondary chords of the seventh of the key of *C* major on the 2nd and 7th degree, with the altered fundamental note and altered third; only the 12th and 13th examples give transitorily some modulatory progressions to the dominant of *a*-minor; the chromatic alterations being effected, of course, in the same part (alto) to avoid false relation. The cantus firmus would allow still different ways of treatment; those given here however, are sufficient to aid the student in working out his exercises.

It is not positively necessary (as shown in examples 1 and 2), to make use of triads only in the following exercises.

Exercises.

17. 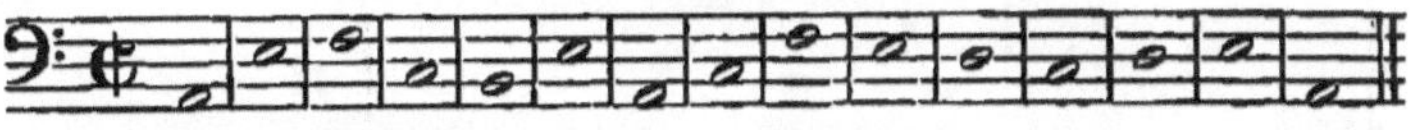

18. 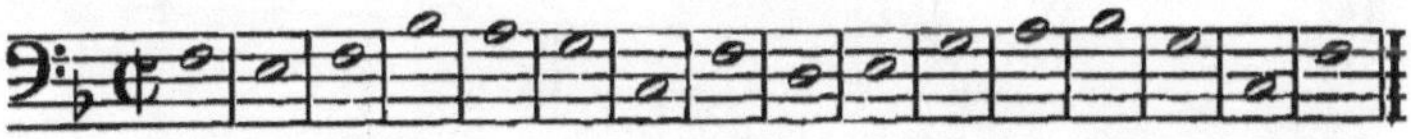

19. 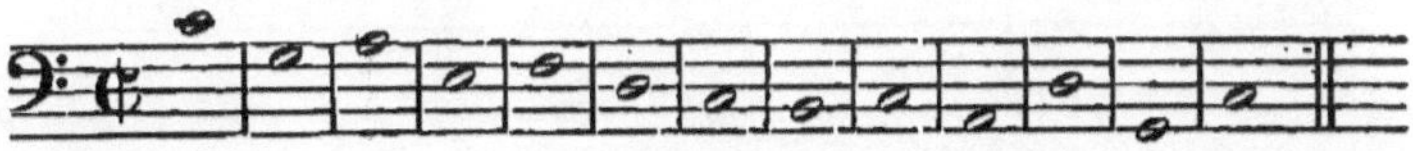

20. 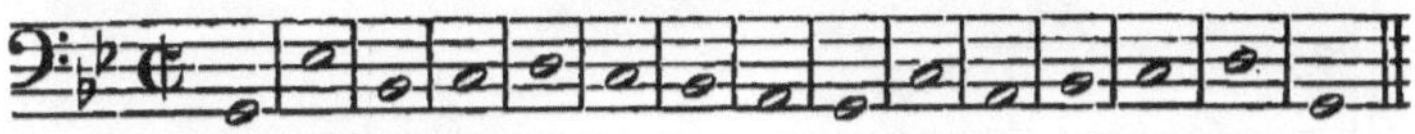

21. 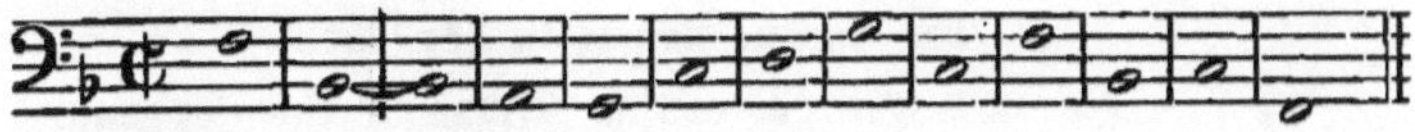

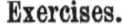

22. 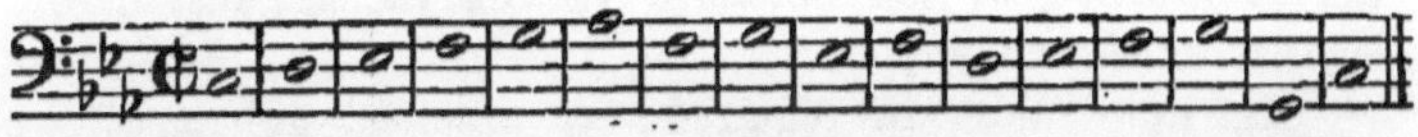

23. 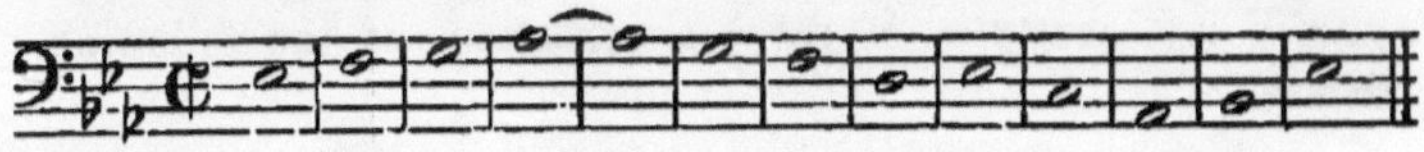

24. 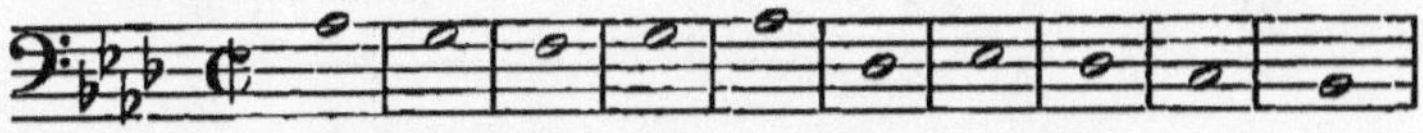

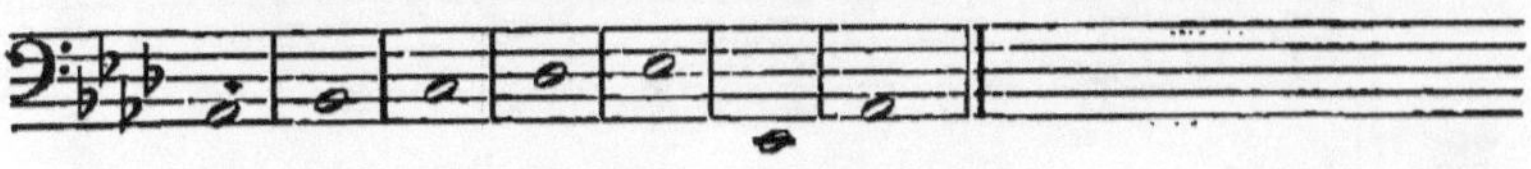

25. 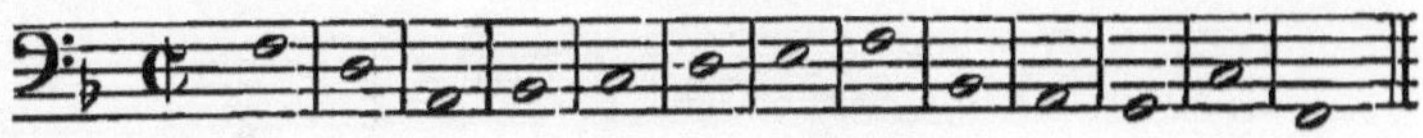

For the guidance of the student the commencement of the exercise No. 17 may be as follows:

26.

etc.

etc.

etc.

etc.

etc.

etc.

etc.

etc.

The Cantus firmus in Soprano.

§ 2. We now give a cantus firmus in the Soprano. Here the progression of the bass will require the greatest care. (See Manual of Harmony § 61.)

No new rules are required; as practical guidance, we here give a few examples of the commencement of the following cantus firmus.

27.   etc.

28.

etc.

Exercises.

34.

35.

36.

The exercises No. 30. 32. 34. 36. contain the leading notes of their respective minor-keys, and have of course to be worked in minor.

The Cantus firmus in the Middle Parts.

§ 3. When the cantus firmus is placed in the alto and tenor, the task becomes considerably more difficult than when the former lies in extreme parts. Though the progression of the middle parts has to be melodious and independent, still, when the cantus firmus is placed in one of the middle parts, it will be forced by its circumscribed position to a more quiet and confined progression, and cannot obtain that free melodious formation which the soprano and bass ought to receive. Therefore when the principal melody, the cantus firmus, lies in one of the middle parts, we have to consider the soprano especially. This highest part may never adopt the quiet confined character of a middle part. (Compare Manual of Harmony § 61.) The treatment of the cantus firmus placed in the alto in the following manner in No. 37, would be most clumsy.

37.

The above exercise would be somewhat improved by changing the tenor with the soprano; we reproduce it in this form in No. 38.

38.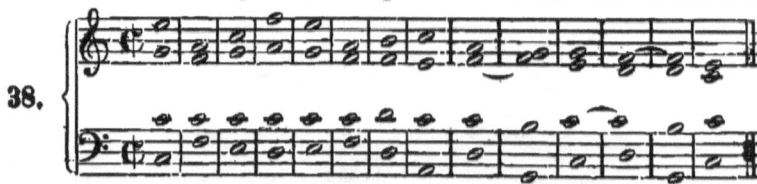

We add two more workings out of the same cantus firmus in the alto, in which the tenor progresses more melodiously than in No. 38, where it is only a replacement of the soprano, intentionally formed in an awkward manner.

39 a.

or:

39 b.
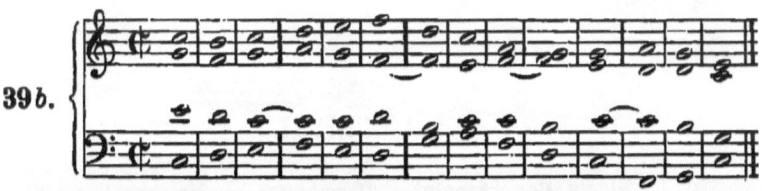

We now give some exercises for the treatment of the cantus firmus in alto and tenor. It is not advisable to spend too much time on these exercises. The student can only obtain complete certainty in four-part writing later on, when he has mastered more complicated contrapuntal problems.

Exercises.

Cantus firmus in the Alto.

Cantus firmus in the Tenor

CHAPTER II.

Florid Counterpoint.   (Two notes against one.)

§ 4.   In simple counterpoint the parts can only progress independently with respect to melody; in florid counterpoint however,
the independence of parts is considerably heightened by the freer
rhythmical movement of one or more parts against the cantus firmus.
Formerly one allowed 2, 3, 4, 6, even 8 notes to one of the cantus
firmus, and practised this — at the beginning — by adding one florid
part only. Here it will suffice if the student first learns to write
two notes, and later on four, against one of the cantus firmus;
as all other species — in common or triple time — will have to
be reduced to these two. Still we adhere to the procedure of at
first giving one florid part only; although in practice it is more
generally the case, that more than one part employs motion in
turn, or simultaneously. Though it may prove more difficult to
produce movement in one part only, still, just by this means the
attention ist fixed upon the proper progression of the individual
parts. After the student has had sufficient practice in the manage-
ment of each part alone, it will be an easy matter for him to work
with freedom and certainty a partly simultaneous, partly alternative
florid counterpoint, between the different parts.

We now commence our studies by giving two notes to the
bass, against one of the cantus firmus. *Each note of the counterpoint has to be purely harmonic.* In rare cases only, a suspension
well prepared by leap, may be employed. This may take place

either at the beginning, or shortly before the end of the exercise, for instance:

Commencement.   Close.

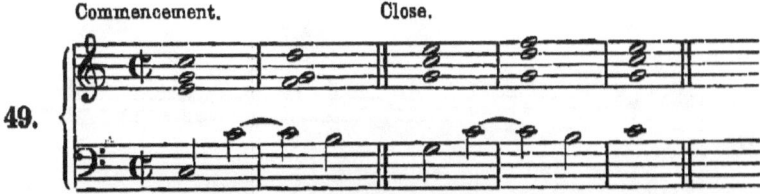

49.

In the middle of a movement, the introduction of a suspension, even if well prepared, would make a disagreeable impression, as it interrupts the motion of the bass. That a suspension in the bass can only as a rule, be employed before the third of a chord, has been shown in the "Manual of Harmony".

If then a suspension, as disturbing the motion in the bass has to be used with care only, it stands to reason, that the tying of a note of one chord to the same note in another harmony, has to be avoided altogether. Only the three following rules will therefore be available.

1. A Leap from one to another note of the same chord.
2. The Passing Seventh, occurring between the root of a chord and the third below it.
3. The fundamental note of a chord of the seventh, following a chord of the sixth.

These three methods we see employed in the three following bars, namely: method first in the first bar, method second in the second, method third in the third bar.

The last bar of No. 50 b shows, that we may leave out the third of a chord on the second half of a bar; but it may never be omitted in the first half, and only very exceptionally in a chord of the seventh.

In a few exceptional cases the fundamental note of a chord of the seventh can follow the root of a chord, provided that retarded parallel octaves are not merely hidden by so doing.

Ex. 51ᵃ cannot be found fault with; No. 51ᵇ is quite inadmissable.

51.

The bare consecutive fifths and octaves, which occur between the strong beats in Ex. 51 b., are not sufficiently concealed by the leap of a sixth on the weak beat of the first bar. A counterpoint, such as the one in No. 52, would be entirely unallowable.

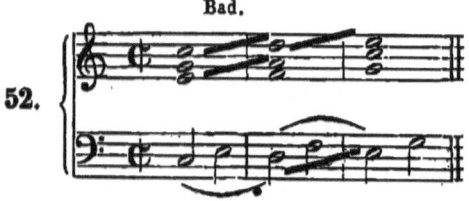

Bad.

52.

Still in a few instances, the parallel octaves are suspended by the motion. This is the case when the bass, bearing a chord of the sixth, is succeeded by the fundamental note of the chord of the seventh. If contrary motion is employed, especially in connection with two chords of the seventh (53ᵃ), the effect would be a good one.

53.

§ 5. More than three notes belonging to the same chord and proceeding in the same direction should not be given to the counterpoint. Consequently the progression of the bass in Ex. 54 is bad.

54.

Here the bass moves in the same direction; the notes *C*, *E*, *G*, *B* (chord of the seventh on the first degree of *C* major;) after that, *C*, *A*, *F*, *D* (II_7) *A*, *F*, *D*, *B* (vII^0_7) and *F*, *D*, *B*, *G* (v_7). Such progressions should always be avoided. Towards the end, (last bar but one), the bass may very well make a leap of an octave, best however from below, but also from the higher to the lower octave. A leap of an octave — preferably upwards — can also be employed advantageously, at the beginning of the exercise (first bar). In the middle of a movement, progressions of octaves should only be used exceptionally.

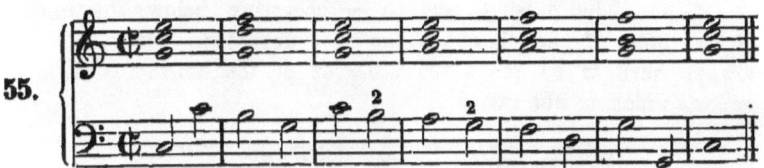

55.

§ 6. The last bar seldom if ever contains motion, the first bar can also do without it; occasionally the bass may commence on the second beat of the bar.

or:

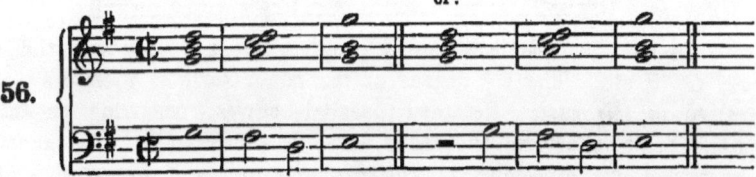

56.

Any other passing note except that of the seventh descending from the root of the chord, is not at all admissable. The progression of the bass in No. 57ᵃ is bad, but the one at 57ᵇ is good.

a. Bad.   *b.* Good.

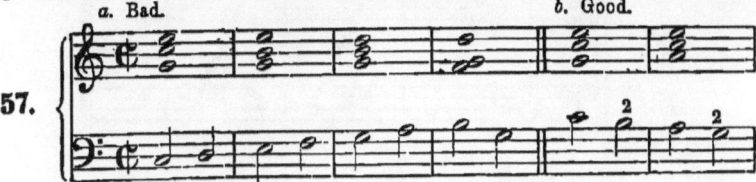

57.

As the passing seventh allows the bass only diatonic progression, and considering that this part must mostly move by leap, one can occasionally give two chords to one note of the cantus firmus, provided that if by so doing, it affords the bass an opportunity of moving diatonically, and provided also that the progression of harmony be clear, natural and comprehensible, as demonstrated in the following Ex. 58 NB.

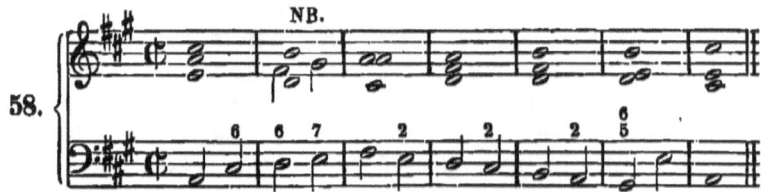

§ 7. The passing seventh — occurring below the fundamental note of the chord on the first degree in minor, — will always have to be the seventh degree of the *descending* scale in minor, which is not raised.

In Ex. 59, the bass cannot progress in any other way than: *A, G, F* etc. The 7th degree of the minor scale is therefore not raised *in this case*. Retarded parallel-octaves, occurring on the weak beats in several successive bars, as shown in Ex. 60, cannot be permitted, especially as the regularity and stiff progression of the extreme parts is not good.

The retarded parallel-octaves however, between the strong beat of one bar, and the weak beat of the next, are permissible and completely covered by the intermediate notes.

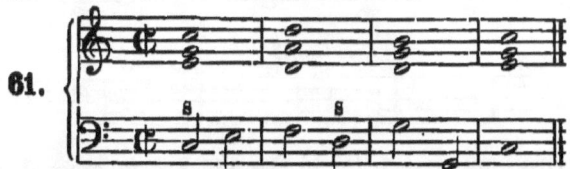

61.

Between the weak beats of two successive bars, the parallel-octaves, concealed and retarded by the first note of the second bar, *can only occur once.* Example 62 is not to be censured, but Example 63, showing the same beginning, is bad, on account of its further progression.

Not to be blamed.

62.

Not good.

63.

§ 8. We now give to the student some exercises of a counterpoint of two notes against one of the cantus firmus, which latter can be used for alto as well as for tenor.

The Cantus firmus is in the Soprano.

NB.[1]

64.

At NB.[1], the seventh (*F*) in the alto has to proceed upwards, on account of the passing seventh (*F*) in the bass, which must descend. Likewise at NB.[2], the seventh (*F*) in the alto has to proceed upwards, as the bass leaps to *E*, the original note of resolution. (See Manual of Harmony § 43.)

The retarded parallel-octaves, between the extreme parts NB. which fall on the weak beat, are admissible. (See Example 62.)

Now follows the counterpoint for the cantus firmus in the alto; see Example No. 44.

This example requires no further explanation. In Example 66 we give a working out of the cantus firmus, No. 48, but in the tenor and with two notes in the counterpoint.

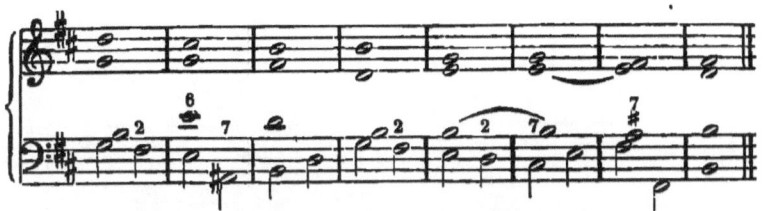

The beginning of example 65 might also be done as follows:

67.

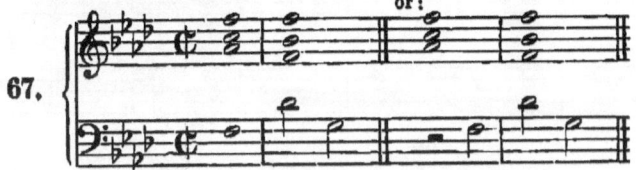

In order to give the student as much practical guidance as possible, we add a few workings of the following cantus firmus; only the last of them contains a modulatory deviation.

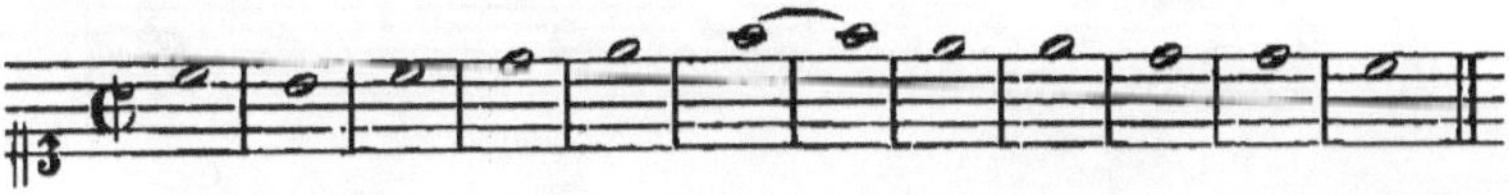

68. 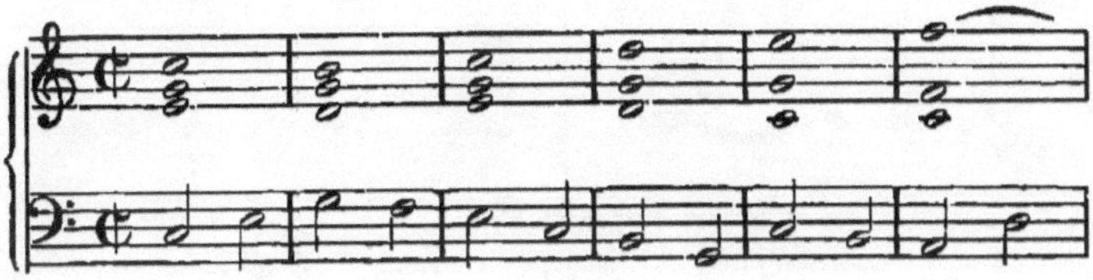

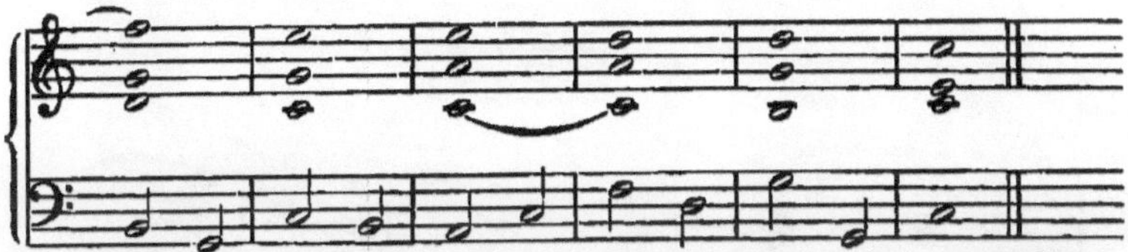

69. 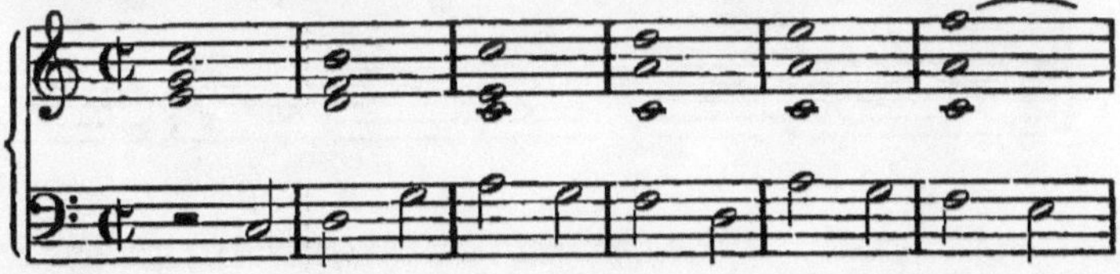

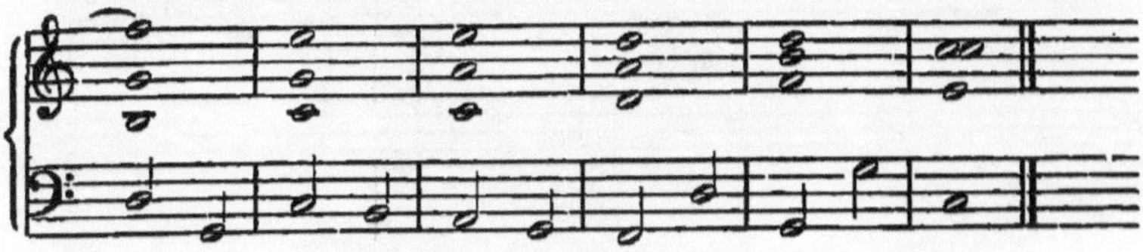

or:

73.

NB.

One chromatic passing note, as at NB. in Ex. 73, can be used occasionally; such a note then takes the character of an altered tone, ascending from the natural tone. But this does not give an actual modulatory effect. The commencement of the foregoing cantus firmus can be treated in the following manner:

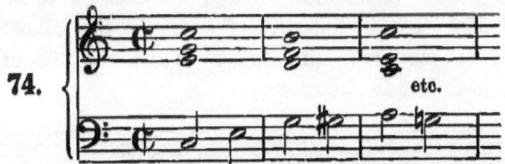

74.   etc.

Several of such chromatic progressions however, should not be employed one after the other, as in this case the progressions of the parts would become what old writers used to term a "*howling progression*". The nature of true counterpoint is of a diatonic-melodic character. The following exercises would therefore be entirely objectionable. (Compare Manual of Harmony § 57. Ex.: 301 and 302.)

75.

Quite bad, because chromatic.

The passing seventh in the alto, last bar but one Ex. 73, is always allowable in any upper part at the close.

§ 9. The student may now work a few exercises, by placing two notes in the bass against one of the cantus firmus. He may choose for the soprano, one or the other cantus firmus from exercises 29—36, and for alto and tenor from 40—48. In the treatment of these exercises in florid counterpoint, the pupil should not try to find support in the exercises he has already done in simple counterpoint; or, to bind himself to the employment of formerly used harmonies. He would not find his task easier, but more difficult. If he kept always to the same harmonic treatment, the mechanical patch-work of putting a second half note on the weak beat, would be most inartistic. One also would soon observe, that what was good and suitable for work in note against note, would often be unsuitable for treatment in florid counterpoint. In attentively noting the examples No. 64, 65, 66, 68, 69, 70, 71, 72, 73, it will not escape observation, that in the counterpoint of the bass, the leap to the fifth of a triad, on the weak beat, has but seldom been used. (Examples 65 and 71.) Now it is not in any way forbidden to leap to the fifth of a triad; the following counterpoint cannot be censured, although it shows the fifth of the chords on the first and fourth degrees.

76.

Such employments of the fifth are therefore not exactly forbidden, either in the use of a common chord or the chord of the seventh, where they form a $\frac{6}{4}$ chord on the weak beat; but one cannot lose sight of the fact that the frequent use of the fifth on the second half of the bar, gives a feeble, halting and awkward character to the counterpoint. We warn the pupil therefore, against too frequent an employment of this progression. For this reason Example 77 is not to be recommended, although it does not violate any of the foregoing rules.

77.

The fifths of the common chords, marked with * in Ex. 77, are easily avoidable as shown in Example 78.

78.

At the end of this chapter, we wish to draw attention to the fact, that it is not advisable to keep the pupil too long at these, somewhat difficult exercises. In practice mostly mixed counterpoint is employed. Similar exercises are repeated in two and three-part counterpoint. — In instrumental or vocal studies, one would not detain the student at the same exercises until he has mastered them to perfection; by progressing to other new studies, he will learn to overcome by degrees the preceding difficulties with much better ability. As soon as the pupil has attained *some* efficiency in the formation of counterpoint with two notes in the bass, it will be advisable to proceed to the next chapter.

CHAPTER III.

Two Notes in the upper parts.

§ 10.   There are .eight methods available for treating two notes against one, when they are placed in an upper part; viz:
1. The leap to another note of the same chord.
2. Suspension.
3. A tie between notes of equal value, common to two consecutive chords in successive bars.
4. All passing sevenths, descending from the root of a chord to the third below.
5. Leap to the root of a chord of the seventh, of which the bass note is the third, thereby forming a $\frac{6}{5}$ chord on the weak beat.
6. Leap to the Dominant as well as to any minor or diminished seventh, where the minor or diminished seventh may serve to prepare a suspension. *The leap to the major*

seventh is strictly forbidden; exceptionally, in the course of a sequence for instance, it may prepare a suspension.

7. The suspensions of the roots of the common chords of the tonic, dominant and subdominant, when the note of resolution is employed by preparation in a middle part. The root in the middle part should however be a ninth below the suspension.

8. The suspension prepared by means of the passing seventh, if the notes form part of a sequence or part of a series of bound notes.

Note. The reason why the seventh cannot be used for the preparations of suspensions, except in those cases mentioned unter No. 6 and 8, is easily recognizable. The sevenths are dissonances themselves, and as such need resolving. Only the leap into the minor and diminished sevenths, gives strength and power of resistance to these intervals, to support and carry the succeeding dissonance. Those instances mentioned under No. 6 and 8, are explained by the exceptional character of the Sequence.

Examples to these eight rules:

1. The Leap.

79.

2. The Suspension.

80.

3. The Tie.

81.

4. The Passing Seventh.

82 a.

One can write Sequences without hesitation as shown at 81 b.

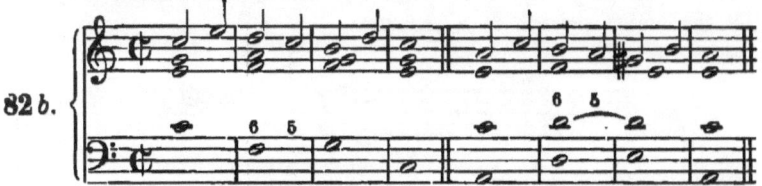

82 b.

The fifth, taken diatonically after the chord of the sixth, is explained as the seventh of an imperfect $\frac{6}{5}$ chord; as the fundamental note of the primary chord of the seventh has been heard just before in the same part.

5. Leap to the root of the chord of the seventh.

83.

This method will be used but seldom, and mostly in such a manner as demonstrated in No. 83. The chord of the seventh must appear in this case complete in all its parts as a $\frac{6}{5}$ chord. Progressions, such as those shown under No. 84, are not recommendable, although they may sometimes be used in practice.

84.

In example 84 a. the $\frac{6}{5}$ chord sounds empty; as the third which is the fifth of the fundamental chord is wanting. At b. the sixth which is the third of the fundamental chord, is missing in the $\frac{6}{4}$ chord. At c. the fundamental note of the chord of the seventh on the first degree appears diatonically, and not as it ought to be by a leap; therefore the effect is weak, although the $\frac{6}{5}$ chord appears complete with all its intervals on the second half of the bar.

6. The leap into the minor and diminished seventh, for the purpose of preparing a suspension, and the suspension prepared by the major seventh in a sequence.

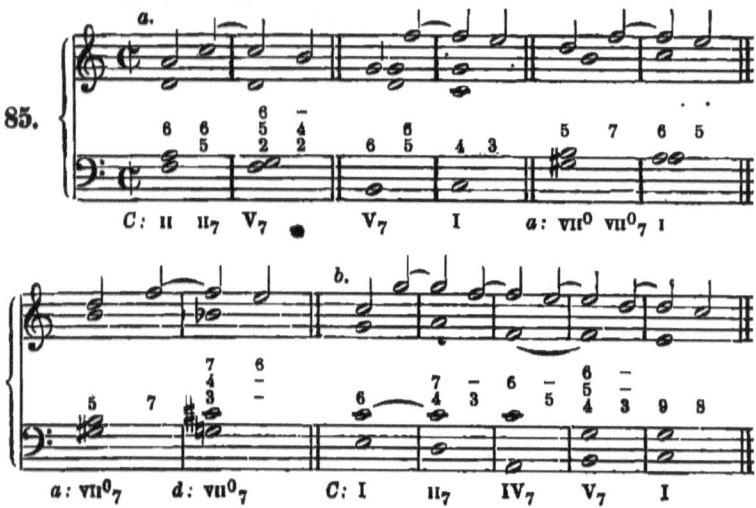

7. The suspension of the fundamental note of the principal triads, although the note of resolution be present in one of the middle parts. (See for reason and examples "Manual of Harmony" § 53. Exercise 257 b. c. and d).

Suspension of the fundamental note of the triad of the tonic.

Suspension of the fundamental note of the triad of the dominant.

87.

Suspension of the fundamental note of the triad of the subdominant.

88.

8. The suspension prepared by the passing seventh.

An instance showing this, is given at NB. of the example No. 87. bar 5—6.

§ 11. We commence our work first with the counterpoint in the soprano on a cantus firmus in the bass, and show the employment of all the eight methods in one example. For better comprehension, we mark the first employment of each method with the corresponding number.

89.

The student need not imagine, that he is obliged to make use of all the eight methods in each individual exercise. On the contrary, he is strongly advised to employ only the most usual ways, which are 2. 1. 4. 6. 3. We note them down in the order in which we consider them most suitable. Therefore the suspension would be the best means, the tie (especially when used in several consecutive bars,) the one least adapted for counterpoint in two notes. More than two successive leaps are not in accordance with the diatonic-melodic character of counterpoint. The following counterpoint would not be advisable just for that reason, although it does not violate any of the established rules.

Not good, on account of too many leaps.

As a rule (in working these exercises) one will do right not to confine oneself to one, but to interchange the most usual means, as far as their employment seems to be adequate to the want; and to make use of the less customary methods, (5. 7. 8.) only when the progression of the counterpoint seems especially adapted for their employment. Only the suspension may be used through several bars in succession; one however should not capriciously amass them. It will be left to the good taste and musical training of the pupil to decide in each individual case, which method should be employed for the movement of the counterpoint. The best proof of the excellency of a counterpoint will be always its adaptability for singing; of course a sound and natural harmonious con-

nection is self-understood. Sequences in the counterpoint should
not be used oftener than three times in succession.

The first four, even six bars of exercise 91 cannot be found
fault with, but to continue them in a similar manner produces
monotony. The use of the sequence at the commencement has
under certain circumstances a good effect; but the employment of
a sequence or sequential progression should not be repeated more
than three times. In this respect the commencement of exercise 92 might be called good, as are also the first bars of exercise 91.

If the cantus firmus itself shows progressions of a decided sequential character in the form of a cadence, it will be advisable,
to take the other parts of the counterpoint also in a sequence, viz:

Cp.
93.
C. f.

or:

Cp.
94.
C. f.

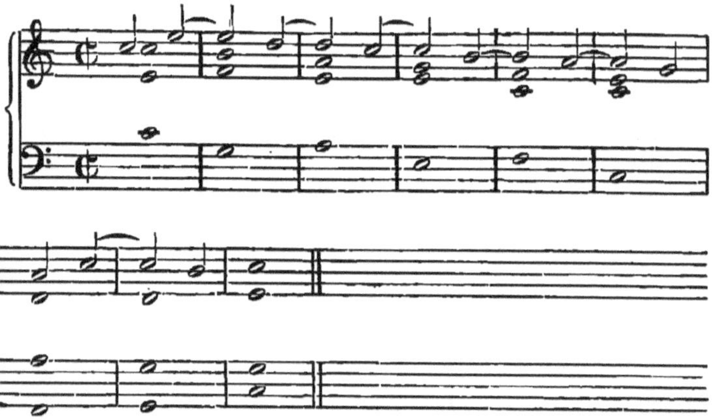

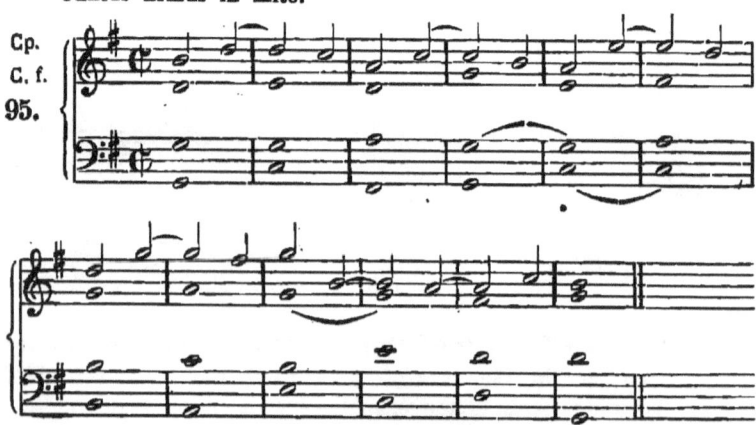

§ 12. Here follow some examples of a counterpoint in the soprano to a cantus firmus in alto and tenor.

Cantus firmus in Alto.

Cp.
C. f.
95.

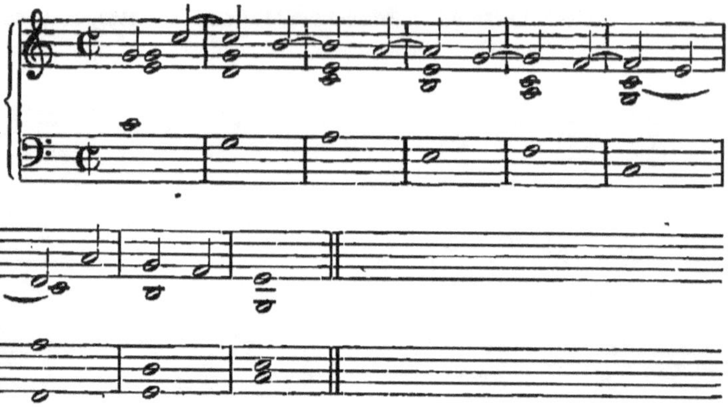

Cantus firmus in Tenor.

The student may now place a counterpoint of two notes in the soprano against the cantus firmus alternately in the bass, alto and tenor of the following examples. If necessary, the cantus firmus of some preceding exercises may be treated over again for counterpoint in soprano.

Exercises.

Cantus firmus in Alto.

Cantus firmus in Tenor.

§ 13. The above rules (§ 10.) will hold good, for the counterpoint in the alto or in the tenor. The seventh method can only be used in the alto. Example 111 shows this case twice in the bars marked NB.

Cantus firmus in Soprano.   NB.   NB.

Cp.
111.

When the motion is in a middle part, it is very much more difficult than in an extreme one. We shall be here reduced to the methods mentioned under 1. 2. 3. 4. viz. the leap, suspension, tie and the passing seventh. It will occasionally be impossible to keep the middle voices within an octave. The transgression of this rule however should not last long, as the exercise would otherwise sound empty. The following treatment of the cantus firmus of No. 111. would therefore be worthless.

Bad on account of too great a distance between the middle parts
permanently.

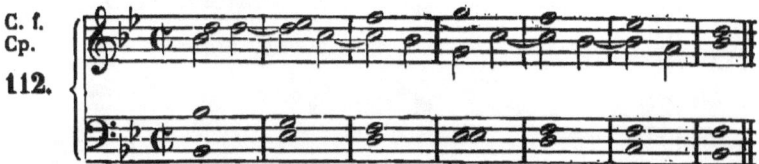

Here follow, for the direction of the pupil, six different ways
of working out a cantus firmus in a middle part.

Cantus firmus in Soprano, Counterpoint in Alto.

Cantus firmus in Soprano, Counterpoint in Tenor.

Cantus firmus in Tenor, Counterpoint in Alto.

Cp.
115.
C. f.

Or these four bars.

Cantus firmus in Alto, transposed to E♭ major, Counterpoint in the Tenor.

C. f.
116.
Cp.

or the following
three last-bars:

Cantus firmus in Bass, transposed to G major, Counterpoint in Alto.

Cp.
117.
C. f.

Cantus firmus in the Bass, Counterpoint in Tenor.

118.
Cp.
C. f.

or the succeeding four bars
with a modulatory turning:

or also:

Exercises.

Note. For alto and bass the cantus firmus will have to be transposed to a lower key.

119.

120.

121.

§ 14. We next work the counterpoint in part alternately, in part simultaneously, distributing it among two or three voices.

A purely mechanical method for this would be to work the cantus firmus first in equal counterpoint, and then to insert the motion in such part or parts, where it seems to be most adaptable. But we do not wish in any way to recommend this manner to the student. He must not put contrapuntal movement into a phrase, without having previously paid proper attention to the movement of the parts. One may allow such a way of treatment to the uninitiated beginner for his first attempts; soon, however, he should accustom himself to conceive the composition in a freer and more artistic manner, which invents and considers the movement of the cantus firmus from the outset in connection with the progression of the parts. The student must continually guard against overloading his work with two or more contrapuntal parts. The simultaneous motion of two or three parts can *occasionally* be of very good effect; at the same time too much movement in several parts fatigues. Now follow eight workings-out of the cantus firmus (No. 120) for the guidance of the pupil. The cantus firmus has alternately to serve for two examples in different parts. The first example is to be always worked simply and in such a manner, that only *one* part interchanges the motion alternately with another; the second richer in movement, is to be worked simultaneously between two or three different parts.

The Cantus firmus in Soprano.

122.

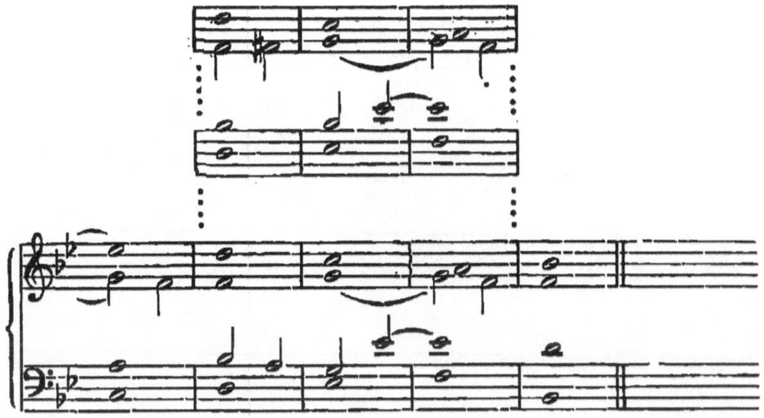

123.

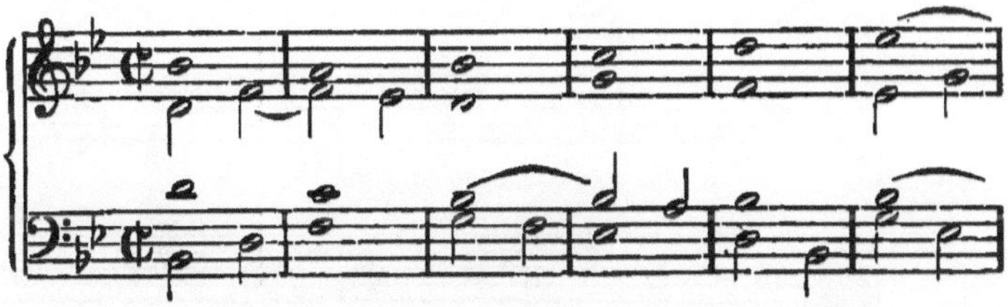

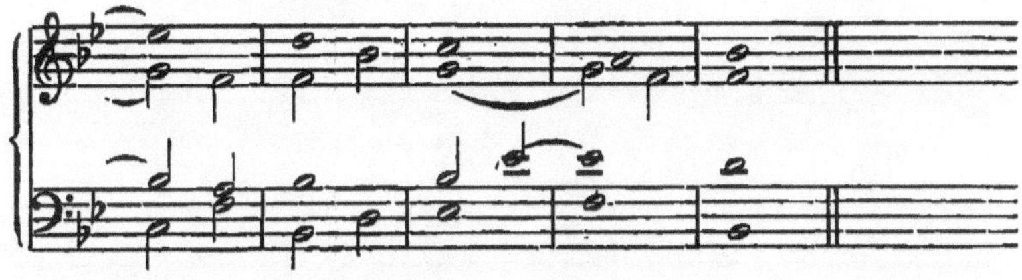

The Cantus firmus in Bass.

124.

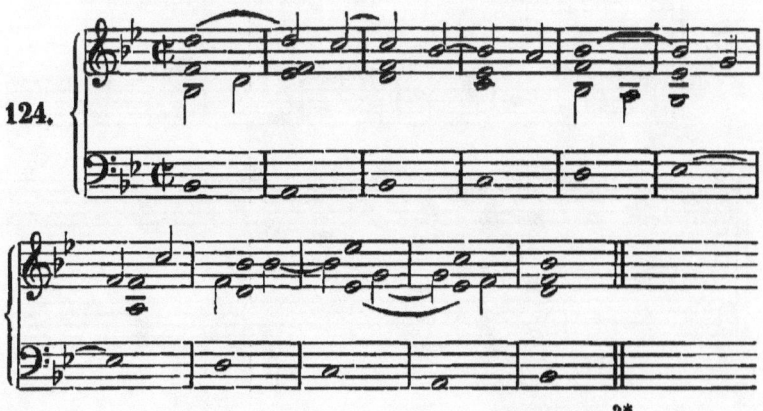

The Cantus firmus in Tenor.

The Cantus firmus in Alto transposed to E♭.

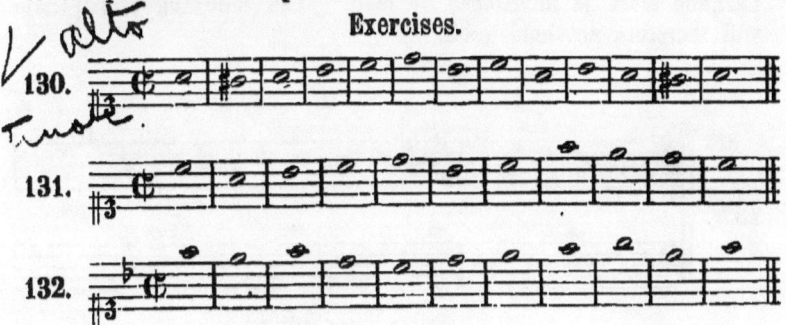

128.

129.

The following exercises are to be treated in accordance with the manner shown in the examples No. 122—129. The cantus firmus may be transposed into other keys for bass or alto, according to the position of the parts.

Exercises.

130.

131.

132.

If considered necessary some suitable cantus firmus from former exercises may be chosen and employed in the manner indicated in the examples 122—129.

CHAPTER IV.

Counterpoint of four notes against one of the cantus firmus.

§ 15. For the movement of four notes against one of the cantus firmus, (four crotchets against a semi-breve,) the same rules apply for *all* parts.

1. The first note of each bar must be an harmonic one.

2. Between two harmonious notes, passing ones may be inserted diatonically.

3. Changing notes (see "Manual of Harmony", p. 153) are to be avoided; in the beginning of a bar they would be incompatible with the first rule, in the middle opposed to the second. But we will not exclude them altogether from contrapuntal work. They will find their place in the more complicated exercises of the canon and fugue and can sometimes produce a very excellent effect. Ordinarily speaking, one will do right to avoid them if possible in all contrapuntal work, even in the canon and fugue; as the note of change no matter whether introduced from above or below, will always have the character of an ill-prepared Suspension, and is therefore not suitable for really "pure harmonic-structure". (Compare Manual of Harmony § 57).

In four notes against one, the tie is not permitted at all, the suspension seldom and exceptionally, and in every case its preparation must be introduced by leap. The following preparations will therefore not hold good.

133.

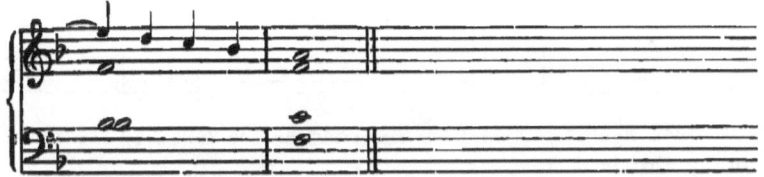

All such preparations of suspensions are bad. Worst of all is the one at *d*, as here the resolution of the passing seventh (which is moreover a major one), is retarded in order to serve as a preparation for a suspension.

Also the Suspension, prepared by leap should be employed but seldom, for instance:

Its employment will be best suited for the end. Many suspensions disturb and interrupt the flow of the movement. Contrapuntal progressions of this kind exhibit, so to speak, a more modern manner than is usual in "strict style"; for instance:

It is just the necessity of the preparation by leap, which injures the diatonic melodious progression of parts. The requirements for really good counterpoint are always diatonic-melodious ones. We must therefore forbid in a movement in crotchets, all figures of chords which do not contain at least one diatonic passing seventh, perhaps also the ninth following the tenth. This diatonic step must moreover be formed by the last two crotchets.

Bad.   Good.   Tolerably good.

Such figures formed from the triad as the following are to be totally abstained from.

137.

A mere circumscription of a semi-breve by four crotchets continued for several bars, cannot be too carefully avoided.

138.

Such a progression as example 138 shows is totally inapt. Circumscriptions of a semi-breve cannot always be avoided; but in such a case a change of the following figures would be advisable, inasmuch as they could be so used to advantage.

139.

By an interchange of such figures one would be enabled at a pinch to circumscribe the following semi-breves.

140.

But even here we earnestly warn the student against this purely mechanical manner of working these exercises first note against note, and then circumscribing the semi-breve by four crotchets. In most cases such counterpoints show their constrained origin very distinctly. Such progressions, as are most suitable for note against note, are not always adaptable in *florid counterpoint*.

The melodic scale ist employed almost exclusively for diatonic progressions in the minor key. The use of the augmented second in the harmonic minor scale must *always* be avoided. In descending, it may be used *sometimes* in very complicated problems (canon and fugue). But at our present exercises in simple counterpoint, we will discard it altogether. In employing the melodic minor scale, we cannot be too careful, that the moving part does not strike a chromatically altered tone, while another part sustains the natural note, or vice versâ.

The minor scale contains in ascending (f♯) and in descending (g♮), notes which do not belong to the chords of the harmonic scale. In employing the melodic minor scale in the moving part, we cannot too carefully avoid using *notes* which are not contained in the harmony of the bar.

141.

C. f.

The F♯ is impossible in the second bar, because the third of the triad of the fourth degree is F; in the fourth bar, the soprano cannot strike G while the tenor sustains G♯. One has therefore to arrange the counterpoint differently; for instance:

142.

C. f.

We now present a few examples of a cantus firmus in minor, the counterpoint being alternately divided between the four parts.

Cantus firmus in the Bass, Counterpoint in Soprano:

Cp.

143.

C. f.

Cantus firmus in Soprano, Counterpoint in the Bass.

C. f.

144.

Cp.

Cantus firmus in Alto, Counterpoint in Tenor.

Cantus firmus in Tenor, Counterpoint in Alto.

Exercises.

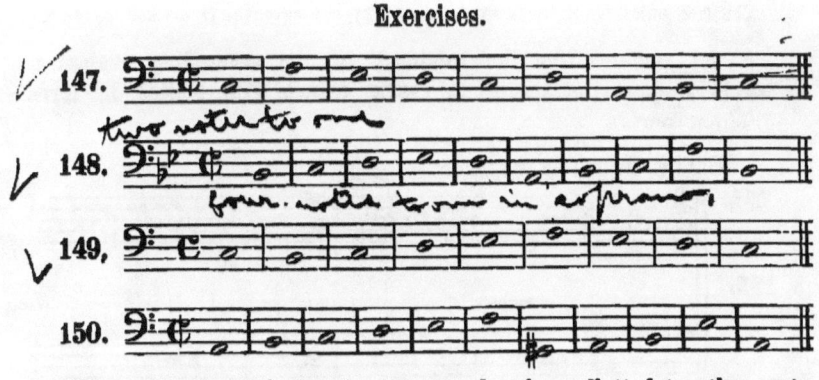

The cantus firmus has to be transposed, when allotted to other parts.

§ 16. In the preceding examples, the pupil has bestowed his attention principally to the development of the part containing the counterpoint: he may now advance to the following studies which occur often in reality. The counterpoint has to be given alternately to the three parts in such a manner that first one, and then the other, takes up and continues the motion. At times two or even three parts may have the crotchets; but this must not occur too often, otherwise the phrase would be overloaded by contrapuntal parts. No new rules are required for this treatment; we wish only to recall to the memory of the student (Manual of Harmony § 56 example 291) that when the counterpoint moves in four notes, the major and minor ninth may enter freely by leap, when they are assisted and attended by the seventh. We show this in example 151.

The free entrance of the ninth, assisted by the seventh, is marked by an *.

As guidance for the treatment of the succeeding examples, we here show the student a cantus firmus with motion in three different parts.

Cantus firmus in Soprano.

NB. Notes may be inserted between the suspension and the resolution (Manual of Harmony § 56 Exercise 289).

Cantus firmus in Bass.

153. C. f.

Cantus firmus in Alto.

C. f. 154.

Cantus firmus in Tenor.

155.

C. f.

Phrases of imitation, as contained in the last bars of example 155, lend a peculiar charm to contrapuntal writing.

Exercises.

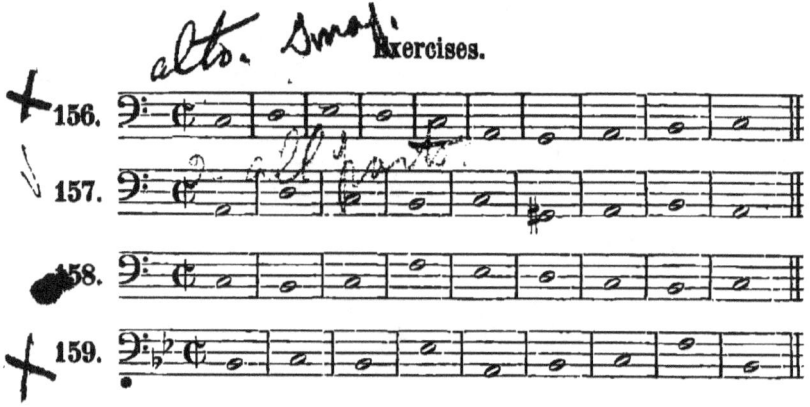

156.

157.

158.

159.

Remarks on these Exercises.

Modulations, and short evasions into nearly related keys, can be occasionally permitted. Now and then a chromatic passing note, or still better an altered fifth, may be used; for instance:

160.

C. f.

Several successive chromatic notes should however be carefully avoided. (Manual of Harmony § 57 Examples 301 and 302.)

CHAPTER V.

Three-part Counterpoint.

§ 17. Counterpoint in three-parts note against note should be worked so that the harmony be clearly recognisable, although there are only three parts available for the representation of four-part harmony. This can be easily effected, as the middle part, (no matter, whether tenor or alto,) affords more room for independent progression. The middle part will therefore be allowed to move more often by leap, especially in fourths and fifths, than was the case in four-part writing; and this is advisable, since by so doing, the harmony can be made fuller. The distance of the alto from the soprano may amount to a tenth, nay, even occasionally to an eleventh. Beginning and end will be best rendered in unisons. The chord of the sixth on the seventh degree may sometimes take the place of the chord of the seventh. Similar motion in all the three parts at once will have to be avoided; but the chord of the sixth on the seventh degree may exceptionally. descend to the chord of the sixth on the first degree.

But the reverse is not so good.

But even this can be occasionally allowed. Though such progressions as follow, have to be always avoided, as they are diametrically opposed to the nature of counterpoint.

Bad.

161.

The chord of the seventh may be sometimes used without a third. (Compare Manual of Harmony § 36, note). Hidden octaves cannot be avoided at the close, when the three parts finish in unisons. Moreover the student may be reminded that all kinds of hidden fifths or octaves will be much more noticeable in three-part than in four-part writing. Therefore the treatment of the parts requires more care. We will endeavour to illustrate in the three following examples, the treatment of a cantus firmus in simple counterpoint in three parts.

Cantus firmus in Soprano.

C. f.

162.

Cantus firmus in Bass.

163.

C. f.

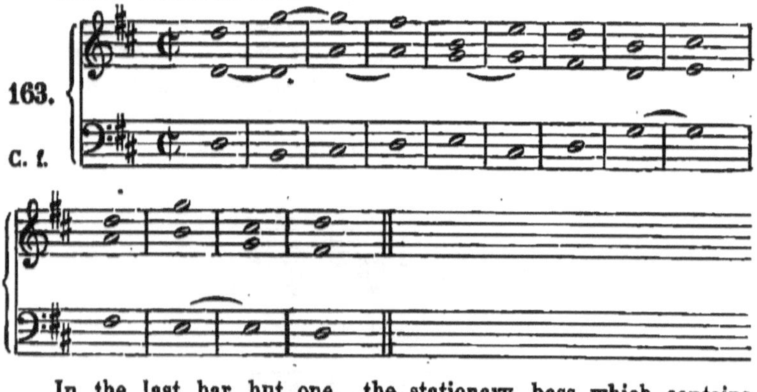

In the last bar but one, the stationary bass which contains the cantus firmus, is made good by the decided movement of the upper parts.

Cantus firmus in Alto.

C. f.
164.

If to this cantus firmus we wish to add a florid counterpoint (two notes against one), in either part, or alternated between both, we shall have to comply with the same rules as for four-parts. It will be more advisable in three parts to use an occasional chromatic passing note when the counterpoint moves in minims, if by so doing the harmony gains in fulness. From this point of view, the G♯ on the second half of the fifth bar in example 165, and the A natural in the third bar in 167, cannot be censured. We directed the bass purposely in this manner to show the student that he may use occasionally, but not too frequently in succession, such progressions. It scarcely needs mentioning, that in both cases, the use of the chromatic note could have been easily avoided, as is shown at the close of the corresponding examples.

Cantus firmus in Soprano.

C. f.
165.

Cp.

At NB. the proper note of resolution D, has been omitted, in order to make the harmony fuller (Compare "Manual of Harmony" § 56).

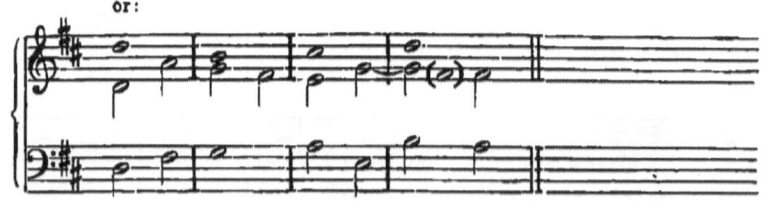

The treatment must be the same if the cantus firmus is situated
in alto or bass.   The student may practise this, with this cantus
firmus, as also with any of the canti firmi employed later.

§ 18.   The movement of four notes in the counterpoint against
one of the cantus firmus will have to be considered also by the
rules, given for four-parts.   Here follow three examples, the cantus
firmus is in the alto.

NB.   Old authors used to employ the whole tone G♮; The use of the se-
mitone G♯ is modern.

The treatment has to be continued in the same manner when
the cantus firmus is placed in the soprano or bass, the cantus firmus
of the following exercises has to be employed in simple counterpoint,
and also with motion interchanged amongst all the parts as demonstrated in examples 161—169.

Exercises.

174.

175.

CHAPTER VI.

Counterpoint in Two Parts.

§ 19. When we have to form simple counterpoint in two parts, we have to commence in unison or on the octave, sometimes with the perfect fifth, and to close by means of the unison or the octave. *No perfect interval should be found in the middle. Unisons, octaves, perfect fifths, and fourths are therefore to be excluded.* We can only employ imperfect consonances: the major and minor, thirds and sixths; and dissonances, the augmented fourths and diminished fifths. These intervals are the most suitable for making the harmonies in two-part writing most concise and recognisable. The minor seventh and major second are not suitable for this species. Successions of thirds or sixths, through more than two or at the utmost three bars, are to be avoided, as contradictory to the character of counterpoint. It is not wise to remove the two parts further from one another than a tenth; in florid counterpoint however an occasional transgression of this distance to the twelfth may be permitted, and the two parts may only be removed so far, transitorily, otherwise they would not mutually assist each other. All hidden fifths and octaves have to be avoided: even to approach the tonic from the leading-note by a hidden octave is forbidden. ("Manual of Harmony" § 59). One cannot therefore write thus:

The close will have to be formed by contrary motion; viz:

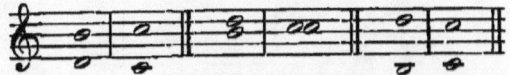

We give now an example in simple counterpoint:

176.
C. f.

We give the subsequent rules for florid counterpoint in semibreves:

1. One can make use of the suspensions of the fourth before the third, the fifth before the augmented fourth, and the seventh before the sixth.

2. The perfect and diminished fifths on the second beat of the bar may be used, after the sixth. This passing fifth takes then the character of a passing seventh, and has to descend diatonically; viz:

3. The fourth below, following by leap, must be avoided.

In return the diatonically descending fourth is allowable, as it bears the character of a passing seventh and is dissolved downwards, for instance:

4. The fifth and octave taken by leap on the weak beat, are permitted.

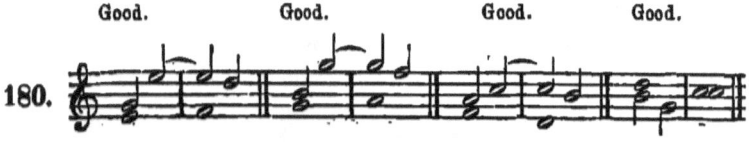

5. A Succession of two major thirds is prohibited.

6. The passing seventh is allowable at the beginning, for instance:

Here follows an example of this kind; it contains a counterpoint in soprano and one in the tenor, both treating the same cantus firmus.

182.

Concerning the counterpoint of four notes, against one of the
cantus firmus, the movement may be sometimes commenced with a
third or a fifth; viz:

183.

As for the rest, all rules already given, also apply here; we
show such a treatment under No. 184.

184.

We subjoin here the following remark. It is not very pro-
bable, that in our time, accustomed to the use of full and rich
harmony, a lengthy and elaborate contrapuntal movement will ever
be written for two *voices*. A short intermezzo in a vocal composition of several voices, (as for instance in a vocal fugue) might often
be of very good effect. It would then serve as a contrast to preceding richer polyphonic figures and so to speak, offer to the ear,
a resting point. We must regard a two-part instrumental composition in an entirely different light; we can see this for instance in the two-part fugues of SEB. BACH (E minor fugue,
No. 10. volume I of the "Wohltemperirte Clavier").

Exercises.

185.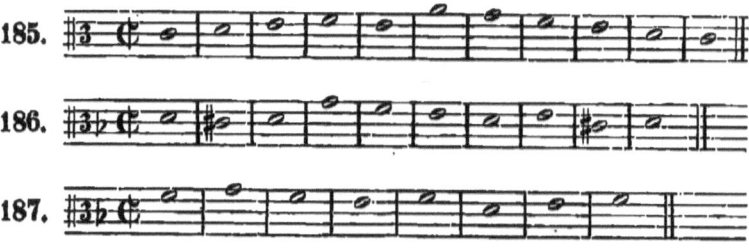

186.

187.

PART SECOND.

Double Counterpoint.

CHAPTER VII.

§ 20. We call a counterpoint double, when it is formed in such a manner, as to allow its removal an octave, tenth, or twelfth, above or below the cantus firmus. We have only to deal with three kinds of double counterpoint: that in the octave, the tenth and twelfth. Older treatises also contain rules for the double counterpoint in the ninth, eleventh, thirteenth and fourteenth; such counterpoints, suitable to be inverted into so many different intervals, can only be formed under such very limited conditions, that they will very rarely, perhaps never, find employment in actual practice. We commence with two-part counterpoint in the octave. We need only add to the rules already known for the treatment of two part counterpoint that neither part should be removed from the other more than an octave, as the effect of the inversion is then lost. An inversion of parts into the double octave would separate both parts too remotely from one another. We give an example of a double counterpoint under No. 188, which could be placed to the cantus firmus in alto, as a soprano and also as a lower part. We will not in future give the cantus firmus only in notes of equal value, as has been hitherto done in simple counterpoint; by so doing the cantus firmus will become less rigid. We shall however have to bestow especial attention on the formation of the counterpoint, so that it is as much as possible rhythmically contrasted with the cantus firmus.

In this kind of florid cantus firmus, a binding is allowed between two crotchets. A crotchet, entering by step of second, may also serve as a suspension. It is quite another thing when

we have minims in the cantus firmus, as the crotchets then stand
in the same proportion to the minims, as the minims to the semi-
breves in all the previous canti firmi.

188.

One will perceive, that only those intervals and progressions
are possible which were available in two-part simple counterpoint.
Intervals such as ·the augmented sixth, which are disallowed in
simple counterpoint, must be excluded in double counterpoint. We
give under No. 189 another example of this kind of counterpoint.
The student will perceive that modulations, which do not lead too
far from the principal key, will be serviceable.

189.

Exercises.

190.

To this cantus firmus the lower part has to be added; in the inversion the cantus firmus is placed in the lower octave, the counterpoint remains.

191.

To this alto the soprano has to be placed as counterpoint, and to be removed to the lower octave, the cantus firmus remains; similarly in 192 and 193.

192.

193.

Double counterpoint in the octave, in three parts.

§ 21.　When we place a soprano and alto to a cantus firmus in such a manner that the soprano, removed an octave lower, can be used as tenor to the bass and alto, we must adhere to the following conditions:

1. Soprano and alto must not be separated from one another more than an octave.

2. They must not move in consecutive fourths, which would form parallel fifths when inverted; viz:

194.

Parallel fourths of this description: will be allowable, when the bass moves in contrary motion; viz:

195.

3. The soprano cannot approach nearer to the bass, than an octave, as it would, when inverted, be placed underneath the bass.

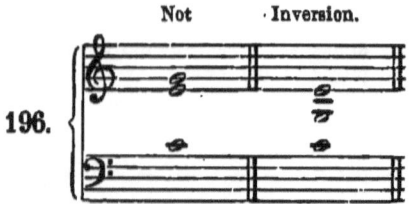

4. Likewise the real suspension of 9—8 ought to be avoided, as the result in the inversion would be, two to one.

When the soprano is two octaves from the bass, this suspension is allowable, as in this case it still remains a suspension after the inversion.

Due attention must be bestowed on the formation of the alto, inasmuch as after the inversion of the soprano into the lower octave it will become the upper part.

Here follows an example of this kind of counterpoint.

Inversion

C. f.

It will evidently remain exactly the same, whether tenor and alto are placed first to the cantus firmus in the bass, as the tenor by inversion into the higher octave appears as soprano. It is only necessary to pay the same consideration to the progression of the tenor with regard to its melodious formation, as was done in the first instance concerning the alto.

§ 22. If the alto has to be changed with the bass, the same rules have to be regarded as those given for the inversion of soprano and alto; with the exception that the suspension 9—8 will have to be altogether excluded between bass and alto, and bass. and soprano, as mistakes against the rules for the use of suspension would always occur at the inversion.

One should therefore abstain from writing:

200.

c. f.

The Inversion would be;

The following suspension would be equally wrong:

We therefore alter the counterpoint of the alto in this manner:

We now reproduce the example under No. 201 with the cantus firmus in the alto.

An inversion of the bass and soprano would be effected in the following manner :

202.

C. f.

First manner of inversion; the Bass is placed two octaves higher; Soprano and Alto remain.

203.

Second manner of inversion; the Bass is placed two octaves higher, the Soprano an octave lower.

204.

Third manner of inversion: the Bass an octave higher, the Soprano an octave lower.

Should we prefer to avoid the slight crossing of parts at NB. in No. 205, (which by the by is quite beyond objection) we would alter the alto, which is a free part.

In all these examples it is quite immaterial which part receives the cantus firmus originally. All exercises are treated by the foregoing rules and principles, laid down above.

In triple time the same rules are to be enforced. For the better comprehension of the pupil, we give an example in triple time; he will learn from the preceding as well as from the following examples, that the fifth of the triad is introduced in all places, with great care, and in such a manner that there may not consequently appear in one of the inversions, an objectionable

⁶₄ chord.   This point should also find due consideration in these exercises.

First kind of inversion: The Soprano is lowered an octave, Bass and Alto remain.

The same kind of inversion will remain, if the Alto be placed an octave higher and the Soprano remains as before.

Second kind of inversion.   Bass and Alto are inverted an octave, the Soprano remains.

Third kind of inversion. The Bass is removed two octaves higher, the Soprano an octave lower: the Alto remains.

210.

We now give the fourth kind of inversion, and to avoid crossing the parts we place the Soprano two octaves lower, the Bass an octave higher, the Alto remains.

211.

Exercises.

212.

213.

214.

215.

Note. For the sake of saving space, we have worked out example 199, 201 a and 207 in such a manner, that the various inversions of each could be shown in connection with the original position. The pupil is not required to follow out this method, as he would thereby only involve himself in unnecessary difficulties. As *accompaniment to the two parts in double counterpoint*, which are to be inverted, he shall add to each exercise a **third free voice** which **need not be inverted**, and which must appear in a different form in the first position of each example.

CHAPTER VIII.

Double Counterpoint in the Octave in Four-part writing.

§ 23. The student can produce the simplest kind of Double-Counterpoint in four parts by forming a movement in such a manner that tenor and soprano can be interchanged. No new rules are required for this. Those given at § 21 and 22 will remain in force here. Here follows an example in which the tenor is so placed to the cantus firmus in the soprano that both parts may exchange places. The alto and bass may be regarded as free parts.

C. f.

216.

Cp.

5*

In the inversion the cantus firmus is in the Tenor; the counterpoint in the Soprano. Both parts are inverted in the octave.

Inversion of No. 216.

In example 216 however, the two parts which are not meant to be inverted, are nevertheless also treated according to the rules of double counterpoint. We are therefore able also to interchange them, (besides those inversions already demonstrated), soprano and alto, alto and tenor, alto and bass, tenor and bass, and lastly bass and soprano, by which proceeding we gain still five more inversions of example 216. But we must here expressly remark that the pupil is not at all obliged to work his exercises *in this manner*; this would cause him a great deal of unnecessary difficulty. He is only required, at present, to work but one contrapuntal part to the cantus firmus; the other parts which have not to be inverted, he may consider as free.

He must work several examples by placing the cantus firmus in another part; and in these exercises he will only have to treat two parts in such a manner that they can be inverted, without any regard to an inversion of the free parts.

The student may practise this problem in the order indicated at example 216. He will perceive by the inversions, that the fifth of a chord has to be introduced with especial care when it appears in the bass in one of the inversions. In like manner the suspension nine to eight is almost always unsuitable. Altogether the introduction and resolution of suspensions requires the greatest care. The employment of the augmented sixth will prove alike difficult. This interval will present itself at the inversion as a diminished third, and not only prove itself a harsh dissonance, but may also give rise to faulty progressions; for example:

The employment of the augmented sixth will have to be therefore avoided, in a $\frac{6}{5}$ chord, as well as in the chord of the sixth. The altered fifth can occasionally be used, as is shown in example 216, bar 5.

Here now follow the inversions of two other parts, which we will demonstrate in further inversions taken from the example 216.

The cantus firmus in the Alto; the Soprano takes over the counterpoint of the Alto. To preserve the voice-parts this exercise has been transposed into F major. Such transpositions into other keys, (as before remarked,) are often necessary in certain inversions when the phrase is meant to remain within the compass of the singing voices.

218.

The cantus firmus in Soprano; the Alto replaces the counterpoint of the Tenor, the Tenor that of the Alto. The inversion has been transposed into A major for the sake of keeping the voices within their respective limits.

219.

The cantus firmus in the Soprano; the Alto takes over the counterpoint of the Bass, the Bass that of the Alto.

220.

The cantus firmus in Soprano; the Tenor takes the counterpoint of the Bass, the Bass that of the Tenor.

221.

The cantus firmus in the Bass; the Soprano replaces the counterpoint of the Bass.

222.

In the same manner other inversions can be worked, for instance: the change of the bass into the alto, the alto with the bass, (having the cantus firmus in tenor,) the bass with the soprano, cantus firmus in the alto or tenor, etc.

The pupil should work out the following exercise. Beginning with note against note in as simple a manner as possible, he may furnish the cantus firmus with a more florid counterpoint in the free parts and inversions. The practice of his own endeavours will prove clearly to him the necessity of the given rules, principles, and remarks on this kind of double counterpoint. The inversions of the exercises should be written down always, in order

that experience may be gained of the real effect of the double
formations of this kind of writing. They will often give rise to
many corrections and alterations of the original work.

Above all the student must give due attention to the independent melodic formation of each part, and see that the distance
of the parts be sufficient to allow for the inversion.

Exercises.

The cantus firmus may be given to every one of the parts.
We exemplify the manner of treatment with two free parts below;
cantus firmus from No. 224.

Cantus firmus in Soprano, Counterpoint in Tenor; Alto and
Bass are free parts.

Cantus firmus in Alto, Counterpoint in Soprano; Tenor and
Bass are free.

Inversion.

Cantus firmus in Soprano, the middle parts are inverted.

223 c.

Cantus firmus in Soprano; Tenor and Bass inverted.

223 d.

Cantus firmus in Bass; Bass and Soprano inverted.

Inversion.

Remarks on these Exercises.

It does not matter if one or the other of the inversions commences or finishes with the chord of the sixth. The $\frac{6}{4}$ chord must be avoided at the beginning and close. Also in the middle of the movement attention must be paid to what has been said regarding the introduction of the fifth of a chord, which when inverted, would result in a ♮. This chord cannot of course be avoided altogether. The student need not trouble himself too much to evade it; one has only to bestow sufficient care on its proper introduction, otherwise this chord may easily sound weak or have a bad effect.

CHAPTER IX.

Triple Counterpoint in the Octave in three and four parts.

§ 24. If in three-part writing all the parts have been treated by the rules of double counterpoint, five inversions can be formed from it, namely:

1. Position.	2. Position.	3. Position.	4. Position.	5. Position.	6. Position.
1. Soprano.	1. Soprano.	2. Alto.	2. Alto.	3. Tenor.	3. Tenor.
2. Alto.	2. Tenor.	1. Soprano.	3. Tenor.	1. Soprano.	2. Alto.
3. Tenor(or Bass.)	3. Alto.	3. Tenor.	1. Soprano.	2. Alto.	1. Soprano.

In these inversions one can, (to avoid disagreeable crossings,) place one or the other parts two octaves higher or lower. In the ordinary inversion in the octave it does not matter, if occasionally one of the lower parts crosses a higher one for a few notes; but this must not be continued through many bars, otherwise the effect of an inversion would be lost. Below the bass or the lowest part representing it, no other part should be placed even momentarily. At the beginning and close the fifth has to be avoided, in order that none of the inversions commence, or close the movement with the $\frac{6}{4}$ chord. In the middle of the exercise, all the rules formerly given regarding the position and introduction of the $\frac{6}{4}$ chord, are to be observed. A suspension nine to eight, has *always* to be avoided. Every part must form an independent melody, as each of them inverted in its turn in the soprano, will become an upper part. For this reason the resting of one part for any length of time on the same note would be impracticable, unless it be purposely meant as a pedal. This however would not sound well in three parts. We here give an example of triple counterpoint with all the inversions. The cantus firmus is first placed in the bass.

First inversion. The Alto is placed an octave lower and forms the Bass.

Second inversion.   The Alto is placed in the higher octave
and becomes the Soprano.   This and the next inversion ought to
be transposed to the key of *G.* to render them more practicable
for the voices.

Third inversion.   The Soprano is placed an octave lower, Bass
and Alto an octave higher; the Soprano now forms the Bass.

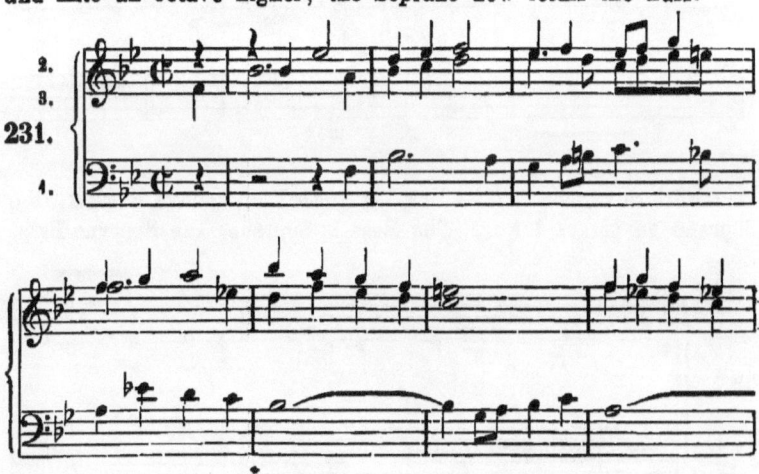

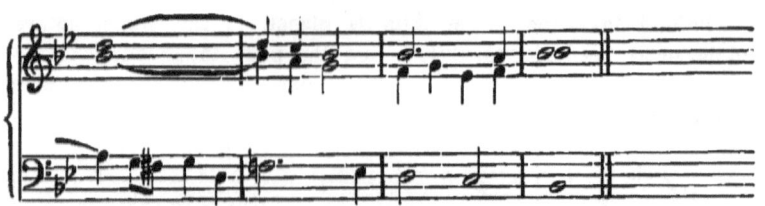

Fourth inversion. The Bass is placed an octave higher; the Alto forms the Bass in this inversion.

Fifth inversion. The Bass is placed an octave higher, the Soprano an octave lower. The Bass is Soprano, the Soprano Bass.

Exercises.

After the student has worked out the cantus firmus of these exercises, he may try to invent by himself similar phrases which would allow five inversions.

If it be intended in four-part writing to place the three upper parts in triple-counterpoint in the octave to a cantus firmus, the task would be in some respects rather easier than in the foregoing three-part exercises.

As none of the three upper parts would have to form the bass in any of the inversions, we could introduce the fifths everywhere. Even the suspension of the ninth to the octave can be brought into requisition, as we show in the subjoined example, bars five and seven. An occasional crossing of the parts quickly passing in one of the five inversions would not be of any moment, especially if it were in the middle parts. Occasional transposition will be found necessary when the exercises are meant for voices.

The Cantus firmus in the Bass.

237.

First inversion (transposed to *C*).

238.

Second inversion.

239.

Third inversion (transposed to *D*).

Fourth inversion.

Fifth Inversion.

Exercises.

Quadruple Counterpoint in the Octave.

§ 25. In this kind of counterpoint the four parts will allow (excepting the original position) twenty three inversions.

The phrase can therefore be represented in the following twenty four positions. (For shortness we note the parts Soprano, Alto, Tenor, Bass by the numbers 1. 2. 3. 4.)

```
1 1 1 1 1 1    2 2 2 2 2 2    3 3 3 3 3 3    4 4 4 4 4 4
2 2 3 3 4 4    1 1 3 3 4 4    1 1 2 2 4 4    1 1 2 2 3 3
3 4 2 4 3 2    3 4 1 4 3 1    2 4 1 4 1 2    2 3 1 3 1 2
4 3 4 2 2 3    4 3 4 1 1 3    4 2 4 1 2 1    3 2 3 1 2 1
```

We once more have no new rules to suggest; but the strictest observation of all the conditions of double counterpoint already given for the relation of all four parts, will have to be adhered to if the inversions have to prove usable.

In practice such movements with twenty three inversions will

be seldom required; one would certainly never produce all the inversions, (even if they should be perfectly usable,) within the compass of a piece of music.   This would produce monotony.   We
therefore advise the pupil not to stay too long at this kind of
counterpoint.   We urgently recommend practice in triple double
counterpoint; as such movements very often occur in practice, as
we will see later on in treating of the fugue.

Now follows an example in quadruple counterpoint.   To save
space, we will only give the four most important of the possible
twenty four inversions; we here give those in which each part
changes its place.

$$
\begin{array}{cccc}
1 & 2 & 3 & 4 \\
2 & 1 & 4 & 3 \\
3 & 4 & 1 & 2 \\
4 & 3 & 2 & 1
\end{array}
$$

It will be left to the student to write out the other inversions,
he will then see that, provided the parts are worked properly by
the rules of double counterpoint, the inversions would prove usable.
Ex. 216 is also treated in quadruple counterpoint; besides those
six inversions given in 217—222, the student may also write out
the other seventeen.

245 b.

245c.

245d.

245 e.

We show here also example 216 in the inversion $\frac{3}{1}$

245 *f.*

Exercises.

The student may also invent such movements as can be worked in quadruple double counterpoint.

CHAPTER X.

Double Counterpoint in the Tenth and Twelfth.

§ 26.   In double counterpoint in the tenth the question is to invert a part a tenth or third.   The intervals which appear in the inversion, are shown in the following table of numbers.

   1   2   3   4   5   6   7   8   9   10
   10   9   8   7   6   5   4   3   2   1

It is evident that in this kind of counterpoint the succession of two thirds, tenths, or sixths should not take place.   They would result, in the inversion in parallel octaves, unisons or fifths.

Inversion.

The fourth and the seventh can only be used in passing in such a way that the fourth proceeds to the fifth, which in the inversion naturally becomes a seventh to a sixth; for instance:

Inversion.

Inversion.

The suspension of the ninth is resolved in this way:

Inversions.

It is clear, that in the double counterpoint in the thent only contrary and oblique motion can serve the purpose, as those intervals generally used in parallel motion: thirds, sixths, and tenths have to be excluded.

Older treatises put forward a considerable number of rules concerning those intervals, suspensions and progressions which were to be evaded or permitted. All those rules are unquestionably correct, but in most cases they serve, as many years of experience has taught us, only to embarrass the student. We, on the other hand, suggest but *one simple rule* for the double counterpoint in the tenth; and this contains all that is required for its formation.

> To the higher part write a lower, so that both proceed together
> in thirds
>
> And to the lower part write an upper, so that both proceed together
> in thirds.

The harmony of all four parts as a whole must be clear and natural.

Now provided the rules, relating to double counterpoint in the octave have been taken into account, one will be able to invert a phrase treated in this manner, in the tenth. Regard the subjoined example.

C. f.

249.

Cp.

Here it will be seen that we have so arranged the lower part with the cantus firmus, that we may add thirds above it; in like manner we may also write thirds below the upper part. As the parts are treated according to the laws of double counterpoint in the octave, we shall now be enabled to invert each part a tenth or what is equivalent a third. We show this in the following examples.

First kind of inversion. The upper part is placed a tenth (or third) lower, the lower part remains.

250.

To this and also to the succeeding inversions, one or two free parts have of course to be added, as in practice such counterpoints formed by two parts only, could not be used.

Second kind of inversion. The upper part remains, the under part is placed a third (or tenth) higher.

251.

Third kind of inversion. Both parts are placed a third (or tenth) higher.

Fourth kind of inversion. The upper part is placed a tenth lower, the lower one a tenth higher.

We can treat this example in three parts in the following way, which contains one part worked in double counterpoint in the octave.

We only give the commencements; the student may for practice, write out the whole example as well as the inversions.

First manner.

253 *b.*

Second manner.

253 *c.*

It is also practicable to add to the counterpoint another free part, which need not be inverted; but then the free part requires to be replaced as middle or lower part in each inversion.

In the same manner one can add two free parts to the two parts in the double counterpoint in the tenth, and reconstruct them in each inversion.

We demonstrate this by furnishing example 250 (the first inversion of 249) with *one* free upper part, and example 253 a (fourth inversion) with *two* free parts (Soprano and Tenor).

253 *d.*

We transpose the inversion of 253 *a* to A minor as more adaptable for voices.

253 *e*.

It is self-understood that this kind of double counterpoint can also be treated in four parts by combining the above two additional parts in thirds, for instance:

254.   etc.

We have shown this already in example 249 with small notes, and give now three inversions of this little phrase. This will prove beyond doubt that no other triple or quadruple counterpoint exists except that in the octave.

We here add another example of the employment of such double counterpoint. This is the "Stretto" (Engführung) in SEB. BACH's fugue in *B* flat-minor (Wohltemperirtes Clavier, Th. II).

258.

The student may now endeavour to compose little movements in double counterpoint in the Tenth on his own account.

Double Counterpoint in the Twelfth.

§ 27. In comparing the following tables of numbers and notes, one will perceive that by inversion the unisons and octaves will be changed into twelfths and fifths, the eleventh into the second, the tenth into the third, and vice versa.

As the sixth by inversion, becomes a seventh it must be always prepared, and descend one step diatonically; as a descending
passing note it need not be prepared; for instance:

Prepared sixth.   Unprepared passing sixth.

Inversions.

The double counterpoint in the twelfth is based essentially on
the progression of thirds or tenths.   This monotonous combination
requires to be cleverly concealed, by giving the contrapuntal part
a free movement.   We will show this to the student in the following example.   One generally adds to the notes of the cantus firmus
only the third or tenth.

259.

C. f.

Therefore the counterpoint is formed in such a manner, that
the progression of thirds and tenths is as much as possible
covered; for instance:

260.

C. f.

From this little phrase we could be able to form the four following inversions.

First inversion. The counterpoint is placed a twelfth lower, the cantus firmus remains.

Second inversion. The cantus firmus is placed a twelfth higher, the counterpoint remains.

The third kind of inversion would correspond to the first. The cantus firmus is placed an octave higher, the counterpoint a fifth lower.

The fourth manner of inversion corresponds with the second; the Cantus firmus is placed a fifth higher, the Counterpoint an octave lower.

To these two-parts can be added one, or two Free-parts. We illustrate this in example 260 a, to which we add one free-middle part, and in the inversion 263 a, to which we join two free-lower parts.

The Cantus firmus is placed an octave lower to leave room for the free-middle part.

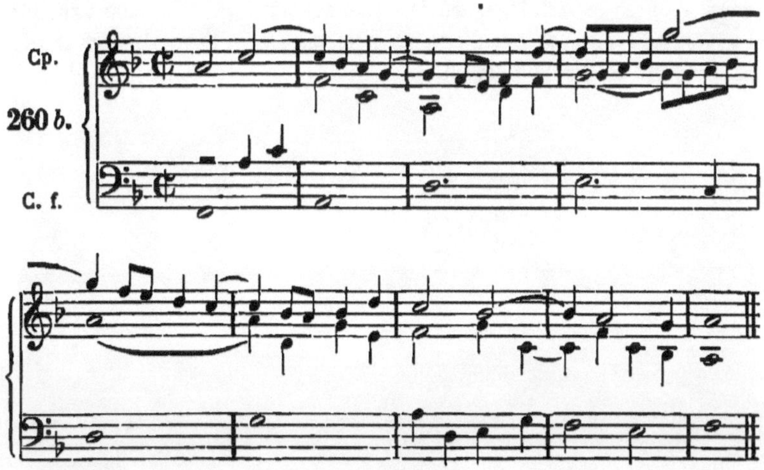

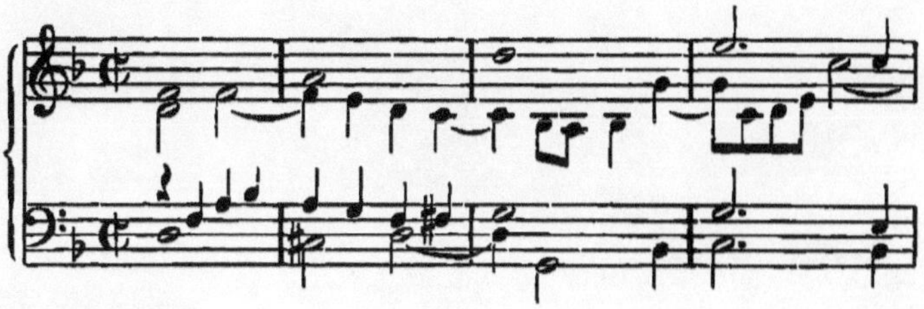

These two free-parts placed a fifth higher will be also avail-able for the inversion of Example 262.

Triple or quadruple counterpoint in the twelfth does not exist, any more than in double counterpoint in the tenth.

If one wished to add to a double counterpoint in the twelfth one or two invertible parts, one would have strictly to follow those rules given in quadruple counterpoint in the octave, which we have already worked in Example 253. All those suspensions and passing dissonances which had to be evaded there, have also to be discarded here. The pupil is recommended to commence his studies in counterpoint in the twelfth, only in two parts, and that even without especial regard to two-part writing. To each example he can add one, or even two free-parts, as we have already shown in Example 260 b and 263 b.

PART THIRD.

CHAPTER XI.

Counterpoint in Five, Six, Seven and Eight real Parts.

§ 28. The more conscientiously all the rules and principles of the "strict style" have to be observed in three and two-part writing, (if the pupil makes any pretention of producing a good effect,) the less strict one need be in movements containing more than four parts. The more numerous the parts are, the more freely can hidden fifths and octaves, doubling of the leading note, the preparation, and resolution of the sevenths, etc. be treated.

If in the course of a vocal composition of more than four parts, the voices be reduced temporally to four, three, or two parts, all the rules and principles of this style will be again available.

In seven or eight parts, it is occasionally allowed to take the two lowest voices in octaves or unisons, for instance:

265.

Let us first elucidate the laws of Five-part counterpoint. Though one could in this species double any of the four parts, still it would be better to write two sopranos, alto, tenor and bass, or perhaps : soprano, alto, tenor and two basses. Experience teaches us that in Choral Societies soprano-voices are the most abundant; next to these the basses preponderate above the tenors and altos.

Naturally, therefore, a better effect would be produced by dividing the more numerous sopranos or basses into two distinct groups, than by splitting up the scarcer altos or tenors, whose parts as a rule, are not so easily heard. For this reason one would place the cantus firmus mostly in the bass, not so often in the soprano, and still more rarely in the middle parts. In florid counterpoint it would be most practical to divide the movement amongst the different parts, and allow it to alternate amongst them. To give motion to *one* part alone, is not advisable in this case. Five-parts, composed of first and second soprano, alto, tenor and bass, would in clever hands produce an excellent effect by its remarkable fullness of sound.

We give an instance in florid counterpoint of Five-parts the cantus firmus being in the bass.

266.

C. f.

The same cantus firmus might be treated in a counterpoint of two notes against one in the following manner:

267.

The same cantus firmus with a more florid counterpoint.

268.

§ 29. For Six-parts, the division of two voices each in extreme part would be most advisable. We then write for Ist and IInd soprano, alto and tenor, Ist and IInd bass. The cantus firmus of Example 266 would be represented in six-parts, in the following manner.

269.

The same cantus firmus more elaborated in the middle-parts:

270*a*.

C. f.

It will be perceived that it is not at all necessary to engage all voices permanently. On the contrary, the effect will be more beautiful if now and then some of the voices pause, at suitable places, or if the parts enter one after another as in the following example:

270b.

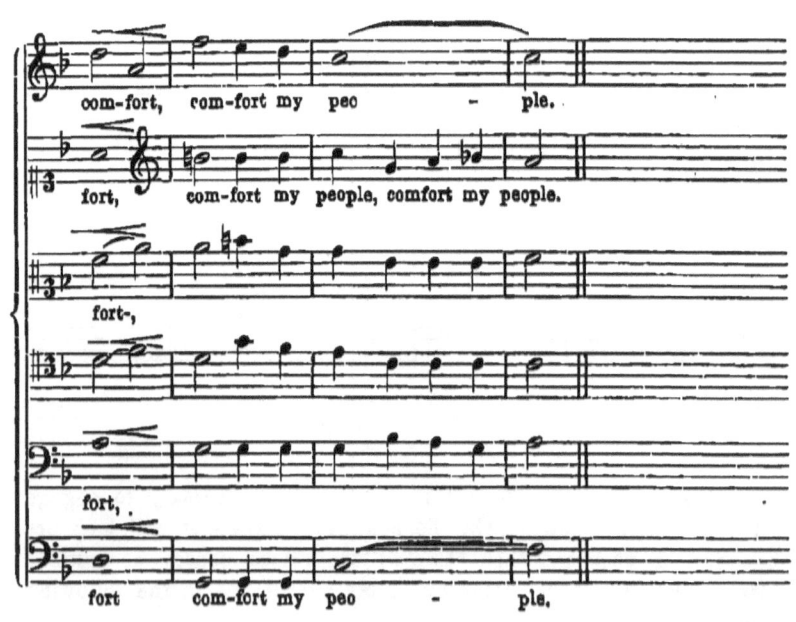

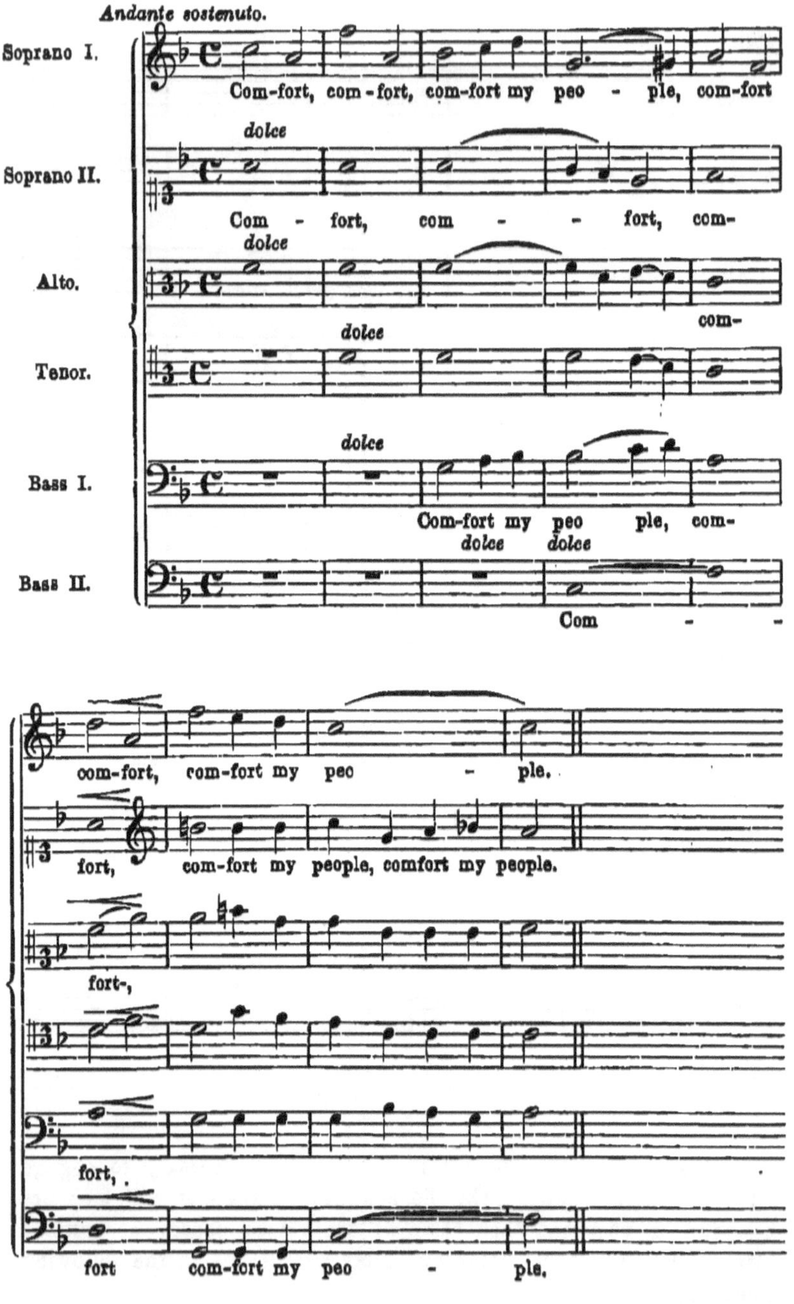
Andante sostenuto.
Soprano I.
Com-fort, com-fort, com-fort my peo - ple, com-fort
com-fort, com-fort my peo - ple.
dolce
Soprano II.
Com - fort, com - - fort, com-
fort, com-fort my people, comfort my people.
dolce
Alto.
com-
fort-,
dolce
Tenor.
dolce
Bass I.
Com-fort my peo ple, com-
fort,
dolce dolce
Bass II.
Com - -
fort com-fort my peo - ple.

§ 30. In Seven-parts we give the two sopranos and alto the assistance of a male chorus of two tenors and two basses. The above cantus firmus would then appear;

271.

The same cantus firmus with two notes against one:

272.

A suspension resolving a whole tone upwards, in conjunction with a suspension resolving downwards, (as demonstrated in the alto at NB. last bar but one) is allowable in pure writing (compare Manual of Harmony § 55). Also the hidden octave above the seventh, between the Ist Tenor and the Ist Soprano (at NB. last bar but one) will be permitted in seven parts; as well as all other hidden octaves and fifths. A succession of a diminished and perfect fifth, forbidden in four parts, is permitted in an ascending direction:  Also octave-parallels are allowable in contrary motion.

The above mentioned hidden octave, between the seventh and the third in the uppermost part, and between the root and the third in an under part, could however be easily evaded by placing (*D* instead of *G*) in the Ist tenor, as last note but one.

We here give the same cantus firmus, with a more florid counterpoint.

273.

Soprano I.

Soprano II.

Alto.

Tenor I.

Tenor II.

Bass I.

Bass II.

One would moreover find it more practicable, in a composition for seven parts, to imagine it as represented by a double chorus, viz: female chorus with two sopranos and alto and male chorus for four parts. It is advisable to employ the two choruses at first alone, afterwards together, as in the following example:

274.

In eight parts, every voice is doubled. One rarely employs *one* chorus for eight voices; *two* choruses of four voices each, which act, in part alternately, in part simultaneously are more usually written. One may sometimes allow the basses of both choruses to move in octaves or unisons; the sopranos of both choruses also are occasionally written in unison; sometimes both choruses are written in such a manner, as to form only *one four-part* chorus.

All these concessions are necessary on account of the extreme difficulty of manipulating eight perfectly independent parts for any length of time. We show the way in which the pupil shall practise this species by an example in note against note, making use of the same cantus firmus hitherto employed in five, six and seven parts. The student may carefully observe that none of the parts form parallel fifths, or octaves with one another.

275.

The same cantus firmus with a counterpoint of two notes.

276.

Should a florid counterpoint be required careful attention must be given to the passing notes, so that they do not lie too near to the harmony notes, thus rendering the passage indistinct. Here follows an example the same cantus firmus.

277.

Soprano I.

Soprano II.

Alto I.

Alto II.

Tenor I.

Tenor II.

Bass I.

Bass II.

C. f.

All the foregoing liberties can be used in free composition, allowing the sopranos and altos, or tenors and basses to progress in unison, or the whole chorus to be treated in four parts only.

Here is an example of this kind.

278.

One would however attain a much better effect, by writing two choruses in four parts each; here follows an example of a double chorus.

279.

It is as well in writing for a double chorus, to regard the voices of the first chorus as I[st] Soprano, I[st] Alto etc. those of the second as IInd Soprano, IInd Alto.

The student may work for his exercises in five, six, seven

and eight parts one or another cantus firmus from the former examples, best suited for this is a bass cantus firmus.

Later on he may himself endeavour to invent such independent, poly-part movements, and to give them the form of small Motets. After having now acquired the rules of counterpoint it will be of the greatest benefit and importance to him, to study industriously the works of the classical authors, such as BACH, HANDEL and others; only then will his studies lead him to real beneficial results.

Explanatory remarks and hints

for

the treatment of the Exercises in the Manual of Counterpoint with especial regard to self-instruction.

---

§ 2, page 8. It is evident that the cantus firmus of No. 34 has to be worked in E minor, on account of the *d♯* in the fifth bar. We work the example as follows:

A working out of the cantus firmus of No. 35 could be done in the following manner:

NB. The seventh ascends, as the bass takes its natural tone of resolution. (Compare Manual of Harmony § 45.)

§ 10, page 24, Example 85. A leap into the major seventh has always to be avoided; it cannot therefore be used for the preparation of a suspension in a similar manner to the minor or diminished seventh. Example 85 b shows the employment of the major seventh descending by step of second and used as the preparation of a suspension, in the third bar in a sequence of suspensions. The dissonance of the major seventh when used as a chord of the seventh with altered fifth appears less harsh; but then the suspension becomes impossible on account of the altered fifth which requires resolving upwards, which would make the note of resolution sound with the suspension.

When two contrapuntal parts move in minims against semibreves in the cantus firmus, one can write the passage in the following manner:

To § 12, page 30. For the working out of the cantus firmus No. 108, we give a few hints; the counterpoint of the soprano requires two minims against a semi-breve of the cantus firmus.

NB. See Manual of Harmony § 53, pag. 131, Ex. 257b.

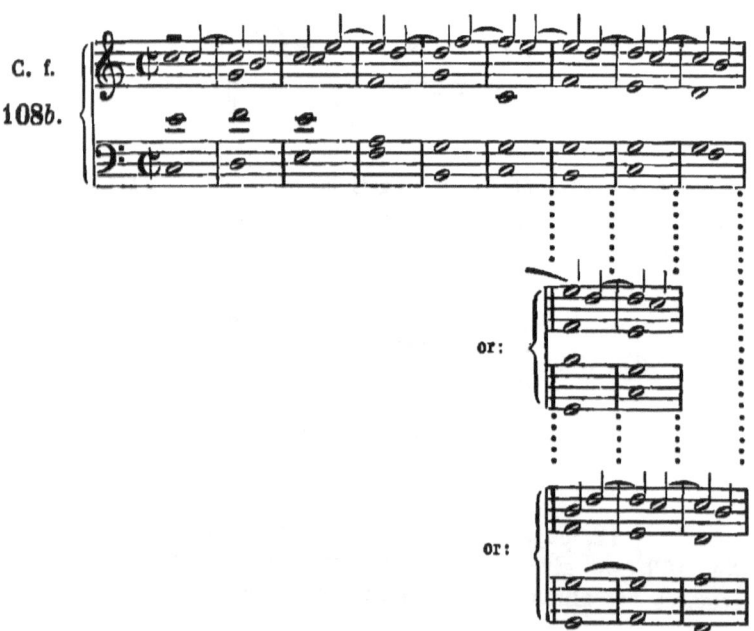

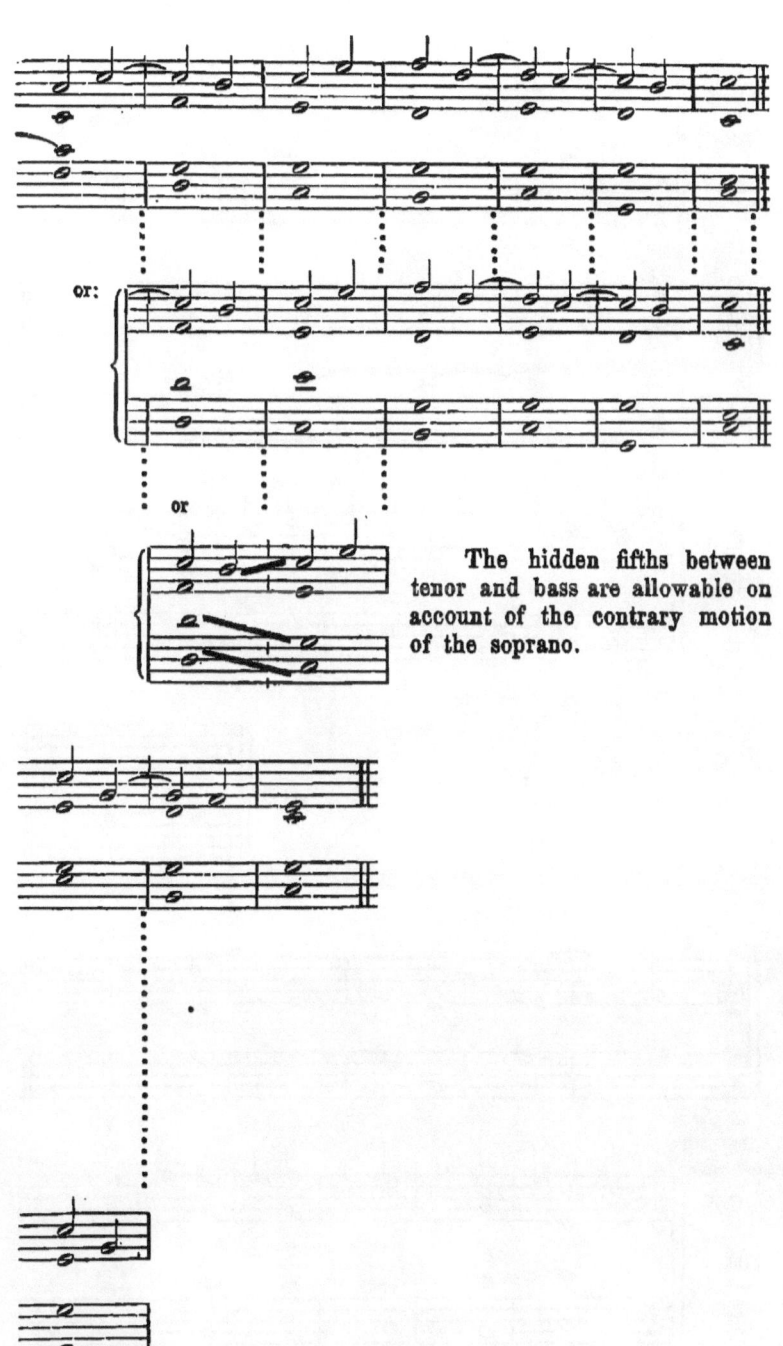

The hidden fifths between tenor and bass are allowable on account of the contrary motion of the soprano.

We add a working out of the cantus firmus No. 100 in the form of a sequence.

NB. See Manual of Harmony § 53 pag. 131, Ex. 257 c.

To § 15, Ex. 134 and 135. Both notes of a leap must be harmonic ones.

To § 15, Ex. 136. In this case the most suitable note will
be the diatonic passing seventh; less so, the ninth passing between
the tenth and eighth. In some cases a diatonic progression upwards
can be used, for instance after three notes of the same chord:

A chromatic progression after three notes of
the same chord could only be available in rare cases, for instance:

or:

To § 22, Fx. 201. It will be perceived on observing this
example, that the distance of the bass from the alto may amount
to two octaves. The careful introduction of the fifth of the major
and minor triad will here be found necessary. It will be advisable to introduce this interval, either as passing note (best on a
weak beat) or prepared, in order that in the inversion, the $^6_4$ chord
does not enter ill-prepared on a strong beat. This can only be
done by the second inversion of the tonic chord in the preparation
of a full close.

In Ex. 201 the fifth of the dominant (*A*, *C#*, *E*,) appears (in
the third bar) in the bass on the fourth crotchet. The fundamental
note (*A*) is struck in the soprano on the first crotchet, and being
sustained, serves as a preparation to the fifth. The fifth itself is
a passing note. In the fourth bar, *D* is sustained in the bass from
the first crotchet; on the third crotchet it becomes transitorily the
fifth in the chord of the subdominant (*G*, *B*, *D*) by the passing
note *G* in the soprano. The same occurs with the *A* in the alto,
in the sixth bar of the same example.

Example 202. The inversion of soprano and bass shows in
the soprano the fifth of the chords on the second degree, (*e*, *g*, *b*,
bar second), the sixth degree, (*b*, *d*, *f#*, bar fourth) and the chord
of the dominant, (*A*, *C#*, *E*, bar sixth) as passing notes on the
fourth crotchet; the fundamental note and third of the respective
chords are each time present in other parts. All that has been
previously said concerning the preparation and introduction of the
fifth applies to example 207.

To § 24, Ex. 228. As in the Ex. 201, 202 and 207, we
would here observe that the fifth of the major and minor chords
are always carefully prepared. Only in the last bar but one (10),

the fifth *F* enters freely on the first crotchet. But here it is the fifth of the chord of the Tonic shortly before the close; and the $\frac{6}{4}$ chord is used quite in its proper place, where it is especially well qualified to indicate the approaching conclusion and to prepare the same. Moreover the fundamental note of the chord (*B*♭ in the alto) is prepared.

To § 24, Ex. 237. A crossing of parts in an inversion can naturally only occur, when the distance between two upper parts is greater than an octave in the original position, as in Ex. 237, bar 3, between tenor and alto. One will observe from the progression of the soprano, (bar 2) that the altered fifth can be employed advantageously.

To § 25, Ex. 245 *b*. Here also the preparation of the fifth of the major and minor chords has been observed carefully; only in the eighth bar, we find the free entrance of the fifth of the chord on the second degree (*c, e*♭*, g*) on the third crotchet. The effect is not at all bad in the inversion, (Ex. 245 *c*) because of the fifth being a *chromatic* passing note of no great moment. The latter could have been easily avoided; it has been so placed intentionally, in order to bring this exceptional case to notice.

To § 26, Ex. 258. If the student places the first 6 notes of the soprano in the two first bars of this example an octave lower, he will obtain an instance of an example in double counterpoint in the tenth, like No. 249.

To § 28, 29 and 30. We add a few more basses, especially adapted for work in more than four parts. The student is meant to treat these at first note against note, and afterwards in florid counterpoint, for 5, 6 and more parts.

INDEX.

Printed by Breitkopf and Härtel, Leipzig.